At Least She Has a Pretty Face

Growing Up with a Giant Congenital Nevus

Lori Clay-Porter

ISBN 978-1-0980-0949-6 (paperback)
ISBN 978-1-0980-0963-2 (hardcover)
ISBN 978-1-0980-0950-2 (digital)

Christian Faith Publishing, Inc.
832 Park Avenue
Meadville, PA 16335
www.christianfaithpublishing.com

Scriptures are taken from the KING JAMES VERSION (KJV): KING JAMES VERSION, public domain.

Printed in the United States of America

"Lori! You can write! I read the whole manuscript yesterday, very well written. There seemed to be two interlocking themes—the nevus and your early years in a Pennsylvania coal area."

—Dr. Jennifer Krup

"I think the book is an amazing opportunity to share your experiences and inspire others with your strength! You are such an inspiration!"

—Carrie Emerson-Coyle

"I think it was great…made me cry and made me laugh, had interesting facts and stories that will help others."

—Carole Koposko

"Lori, I am into this story and I love it… I continue to read and reread. You are so funny and honest and I'm in admiration."

—Cindy Molinaro

"Lori, I have begun your amazing book and your struggle to deal so well with such a condition I look forward to finishing my reading. Thanks for sharing your story."

—Father Jim Parke

Nevus Outreach, Inc., is dedicated to bringing awareness, providing support, and finding cures for people affected by Congenital Melanocytic Nevi (CMN) and related disorders. Your gift is vital to transforming the lives of people with this condition.

You may make a tax-deductible donation today or become an Outreach Angel by making a commitment to give monthly or quarterly.

Contact Nevus Outreach today for more information at:

Nevus Outreach, Inc.
600 SE Delaware Ave., Suite 200
Bartlesville, OK 74003
918-331-0595
www.nevus

Acknowledgments

First, I want to give thanks to God for giving me the idea and the courage to write this book that will hopefully inspire and help others. I want to dedicate this book to my mother Rose Chabanik-Clay who passed away at age sixty-one in 1979. I celebrate her life everyday but still miss her very much.

Special thanks to my amazing husband, Larry Porter.

Thanks to my beautiful babies, Michael, Kimberly, Elizabeth, and Katherine-Rose Porter.

A special thank you goes to the greatest sister in the whole wide world, Mary Katherine Clay-Balog, for contributing her knowledge of me as an infant and little girl and her experiences with growing up in Shoaf.

A special thank you goes to my brother-in-law, Richard Balog, for his major contributions to my manuscript and sharing his knowledge about growing up in a coal town.

Thank you to four of the best friends a girl could ever have, Carole Chabanik-Koposko, Cindy Janesko-Molinaro, Chrissy Cerny-Beissell, and Karen Kuharik-Lemro.

My Nevus Outreach friends inspire me every day, especially Kathryn Rose Stewart and Megan Stewart who I met on the Internet in 1999.

My utmost appreciation goes out to Dr. Jennifer Krup, Dr. Kris Kennedy, Professor Rona Mackie, and Dr. Arnold Oppenheim.

Preface

My deepest wish would be for this book to help not only people born with a giant congenital nevus, which is a very large and very rare birthmark, but also to inspire all people born with unusual birth defects or obstacles in life. Also, to help parents coping with children born with nevus or other related conditions. I learned very early to be compassionate to the problems of others and to accept my own problems and live life to the fullest appreciating each and every day. Moms of nevus babies, please know that your child can live a normal life and that you did absolutely nothing during your pregnancy that caused this condition. I have lived a completely normal life. In fact, I lived a fantastic life with many adventures which I will share in this little book. There are good people out there that are not superficial. I was a happy child, and now I am a joyful adult with an amazing husband, Larry Porter; a son, Michael, and his wife, Kimberly; and two precious granddaughters, Elizabeth Adair Porter and Katherine Rose Porter, who bring me more joy than I could have ever imagined.

> I will praise thee; for making me so wonderfully complex! It is amazing to think about. Your workmanship is marvelous and how well I know it. (Psalm 139:14)

This verse praises God because God created everyone in a magnificent way. God made us the way we are and for a specific reason. When we understand that, then we can have peace that whatever ailments or perceived troubles we have in life are there because God intended them for a purpose.

What Is a Giant Congenital Nevus?

The skin is our largest organ covering and protecting our bodies. Some of us have skin that is vastly different from normal skin. Giant congenital melanocytic nevus. I hate that word; I prefer birthmark. In short, a nevus is a birthmark. But it's really a lot more complicated than that. Giant congenital nevi (plural for nevus) occur approximately once in every five hundred thousand births. A nevus (pronounced knee-vus) is a Latin word meaning birthmark or mole. Congenital nevi are moles present at birth. My birthmark is called a bathing trunk nevus, also a term that I dislike. It begins just under my bra strap and covers my entire back down to the upper part of my legs and then wraps around to the front of my thighs and ends about four inches above my knees. I have two fatty lipomas (benign fatty tissue), one on my left hip and a smaller one on my right side, where a so-called love handle would be. Fatty lipomas are very common with those of us born with a giant nevus. I have about twenty-six satellites. These are small (some as small as a dot and others as large as a fifty cent piece or a little larger) brown spots, and many people with GCN have hundreds of them. I am happy with proudly wearing my twenty-six the largest being the size of a quarter. If you would like to see medical images, just Google nevus and surf around.

Throughout my writing, I speak about hiding and covering up my birthmark. This is not meant to be disrespectful in any way to my fellow nevus wearers who cannot hide or cover it up. I have the highest admiration for these amazing fellow nevites (my friends with super big birthmarks). Very few people that know me are aware of my birthmark. I expect (if this book ever gets published) a lot of my friends will be quite surprised.

I have a nevus that I can hide. So, yes, I am a hider. But it is not because I am ashamed of having a birthmark; I just don't want to go around explaining what it is all day. You see, I, as a giant nevus wearer, shock physicians, so if I pranced onto a beach in a bathing suit, you can imagine what would happen.

Until the winter of 1998, I thought that I was the only person in the world that had a birthmark this large. The internet changed all that when I searched the word nevus online and found Nevus Outreach and Kathryn Stewart. Her daughter's nevus is almost identical to mine, only she has more satellites. It was very emotional for me when I realized that there were others out there like me; so many of them are babies and children. There is no evidence that congenital nevi are hereditary.

There are several types of nevi. Mine is a giant congenital epidermal melanocytic nevus (GCMN). Aren't I special? Giant means, well, huge. Congenital means present at birth.

Epidermis is the outermost layer of cells in the skin. Melanocytic means that it is pigment based. Nevus is a Latin word meaning birthmark. Sometimes, birthmarks (nevi) can appear after birth, but it is extremely rare; they are called tardive nevi. Nevi can be any color from tan to black, but most are of various shades of brown, and some nevi are covered with hair.

Nevi can vary in size from very small to very large or, as in my case, giant. Giant congenital nevi have been described as far back as

1832. Terms such as bathing trunk nevus, vest nevus, cape nevus, and scalp nevus have been used to describe their location. Initial reports of giant congenital nevi were described in 1832 in Alibert's *Monograph of Dermatology* where the nevus was described as a waist coat and drawers, most likely because of the location of the nevus. The first actual medical description of a giant nevus was by a brilliant Czechoslovakian pathologist named Karl Rokitansky in 1861. This intrigues me because I am of Czechoslovakian heritage.

I found out about the melanoma risk when I was twenty-four years old. Although she knew, neither my mother nor any members of my family ever told me. It was quite shocking. I was told by a doctor that I had a 10 percent chance of developing deadly melanoma and that I probably would not live to see my fortieth birthday. The exact risk of melanoma developing in someone with a large or giant nevus is not really known, but recent studies suggest that it is more like 2 percent. That means there is a 98 percent chance that a GCN person like me will live a normal life span. There is even less risk for someone born with a medium- or small-sized nevus.

Just like the weather happens everywhere on the planet, so does GCN. There are people affected by this condition in almost every country in the world. GCN does not discriminate; they appear on every part of the body, in boys and girls and in all ethnic groups. They are most common in people of Caucasian descent and least common in people of African descent and show up intermittently in people of Hispanic and Asian descent. It seems the darker the normal skin pigment, the less the risk of a large or giant nevus. They are not contagious, but I cleared an entire public swimming pool once! More girls than boys appear to be affected, about one and a half girls to one boy, so it is not much of a difference. Cases of identical twins have been reported, one with a large nevus and the other without. Identical twins share the same genes, the same environment, but not the same body protein.

Sometimes, people born with a giant congenital nevus, especially when it covers the spine, can have nevus cells present in the brain and the spinal cord because the spinal cord and the skin develop about the same time from the same cells. The same protein in the body that causes nevus cells in the skin to grow can also cause cells in the brain to grow and scatter. It's called neurocutaneous melanosis or NCM. The research also shows that about one-third of the people with giant nevi also have detectible pigment via MRI in their brains. It may occur and not cause any symptoms for years, perhaps a lifetime, or it may present with sudden, severe, and worsening headaches, vomiting, seizures, or other neurological symptoms similar to a stroke. I have never had an MRI of my brain, and I do not plan to have one. I have never had seizures or headaches, and to tell you the truth, I just really don't want to know.

Severe neurocutaneous melanosis where the nevus cells continue to overgrow with or without associated melanoma is often fatal. Treatment is experimental. I have heard that there have been a few people born with hundreds of satellites and no large or giant nevus. These people have a much greater chance of developing fatal neurocutaneous melanosis.

Recent research may have discovered the cause of congenital nevi! Large congenital nevi form in the womb very early in development, within the first twelve weeks of pregnancy. They are caused by a defect during the development of the embryo. There is no known method of prevention. They think that a body protein called HGF/SF seems to be responsible for encouraging these cells to develop, migrate, and scatter. In myself and my fellow nevites, it seems that we have too much or possibly the wrong type of this body protein HGF/SF in some but not all of our cells. We develop extra pigment and abnormal skin cells called nevus cells. These cells take flight all around, so we have nevi distributed all over us. If we have lots of nevus cells scattered on the skin, there seems to be a good chance that we have the same cells scattered in our brain or spinal cord.

And now for some fascinating news! A Japanese researcher recently developed mice with giant pigmented nevi with satellites! They have too much or the wrong type of the body protein, and they too have a higher risk of developing melanoma. In London, Veronica Kinsler at Great Ormond Street Hospital has taken advantage of the amazing scientific advances in genomics to pinpoint precisely which mutations cause CMN. Now that science knows just which gene changes cause CMN, they have started to design ways to fix the damage. These discoveries might help us to understand and treat skin cancer too.

My mother, while pregnant with me, was visiting the graves of her parents at the cemetery in Fairchance, Pennsylvania. The graveyard was across from quite a large dairy farm. One of the farm's bulls wandered out from behind its fence. My mom hid behind one of the gravestones. She said her back was against the tombstone in the same place my birthmark is; therefore, she thought that may be why I have a nevus. So there you have it, *birthmarks are caused by hiding behind tombstones in graveyards while being chased by bulls when you are pregnant.* I'm sure that many mothers have wondered if they did something wrong during their pregnancy that could have caused their child to be born with a giant nevus. Studies show that it appears to be just one of those things that happen by accident and is just a spontaneous genetic mutation. Nevi are not hereditary. There are many things in life much harder to bear than wearing a nevus. I am very thankful for the many blessings and wonderful life that I have been able to enjoy.

I had no idea of the torment that my mother must have felt because of my birthmark. I had no idea until I had a child of my own. Moms blame themselves for everything, and my mom was no different. I know that she suffered but would never let me see it. By the time I understood what she was going through, she had gone to the Lord, so I never got to tell her.

Several physicians tried to convince my parents to have my birthmark removed when I was a baby. *I am forever grateful that they did not.* Back in 1960, they did not use tissue expanders yet. They would have had to graft skin from other parts of my non-nevus body such as between my fingers and toes. Now they use tissue expanders which are balloons gradually filled with saline (through a port) over a couple of weeks until enough skin has been created to cover a part or the entire birthmark. Then the birthmark is removed, and the flap of skin is sewn in place to take the place of the birthmark. Many adults that have had their nevus surgically removed say that the scars cause them a great deal of pain and look just as bad if not worse than the original nevus. Studies on whether or not this prevents melanoma are inconclusive. Sometimes, the nevus actually reappears, and you can never really remove a giant nevus entirely. My personal opinion is that if they can't make my skin look totally normal and they can't guarantee that it won't come back and they can't guarantee that the keloid scars won't hurt and they can't guarantee that I won't still be at risk for melanoma, then why would I want to go through all of that anesthesia and painful surgery?

I remember going to dermatologist visits growing up, and there were always pictures involved. I just know there are naked pictures of me in medical journals somewhere, probably everywhere. They don't show your face though, just the nevus (I hope). They took them so that the photos could be compared at later visits, and any changes could be found and addressed. It was always unpleasant. I refuse to have any more medical photos taken.

Nevus skin can be very thin in various places because it lacks a layer of fat that pads the skin. When I was about twelve years old, I was running down the stair steps at our house, and I fell. My back hit the side of the wall and somehow cut off a small part of my nevus about the size of a nickel. It hurt like crazy, and there was bleeding, so Mom carted me off to the hospital. It did not need stitches, but it took forever to heal, and it hurt. Nevus skin gets thinner and more sensitive as we age. Because of the fall and then combined by a biopsy that I had in 1988, I now have to wear very soft clothing, and I had to give up wearing jeans. When I was little, I could do anything including roll around in the grass or lie on my back on a hard surface such as an X-ray table. After the birth of my son, Michael, my birthmark started to get a tiny bit sensitive, but I adjusted by wearing softer clothing and taking a small very comfortable pillow with me anywhere I have to lay on my back on a hard surface, such as visiting the doctor for a yearly physical or lying on an X-ray table. Speaking of X-rays, they are not good for GCN people. I only allow the ones that are absolutely necessary. I had tons of X-rays as a child, so I try to set limits. I also limit my exposure to the sun especially since I was always in the sun and getting burned as a child and young adult, not good for anyone especially a nevus wearer.

Nevus skin itches because it does not contain normal sweat glands. There are about two hundred GCN adults on the Nevus Outreach website, and almost every single one of them has a problem with itching. Even the people who have had their birthmark removed have terrible itching problems. I remember visiting one of the many dermatologists that I have seen through the years (I was around thirty-two years old at the time of this visit), and he asked me if my birthmark was itchy. I told him that it was, and he immediately said, "Well, that is a definite sign of cancer, squamous cell, which you most likely have, but don't worry because this type is easy to cure. We should remove this part of your nevus right away."

I said to him, "So you are telling me that I have cancer?"

He said yes. So I started to cry, and then he told me that I should see a psychiatrist because my reaction was not appropriate. It turns out that a member of his family was a psychiatrist, and he referred me to her, hmmm. Well, Larry and I went to get a second opinion, and that dermatologist, Dr. Arnold Oppenheim, told me that I probably did not have cancer and no one could tell for sure without a biopsy.

Having a huge birthmark that covers a lot of your skin can make it difficult to have a positive self-image and to develop self-esteem. Although I struggled at times, I had a positive self-image growing up, and that was due in part to my family accepting me exactly as I was and not treating me any different than anyone else. I had my share of low self-esteem, *bad days*, though as you will read in the following chapters.

Through the years, I never once doubted that I would be married with a family someday. I hugged baby dolls and played house and wondered about who I would marry someday. I remember announcing to my mother one day that I wanted the stork to bring me six babies. I really did not want to go to college although everyone around me said that I was going. I just wanted to get married, have babies, and take care of a house and a husband. That is pretty much what I did until real estate entered my life in 1996. I never had any desire to go to college even when my husband urged me to in the early 1990s. My husband, Larry, has had a major impact on my self-confidence. He is prayerful, loving, caring, understanding, and encouraging, and because of this, he has helped *me* to become the confident *me* that I am today! He has helped me to overcome so many things. I thank God every day for sending him to me.

Here is what I would like to share with the world not just people that look different but with everyone. You have much to celebrate and are entirely unique. Any comparison between you and another person is like comparing apples to oranges. They aren't living your life, you are. Therefore, you should expect the results to be completely different. There are a few things that everyone should learn from people born with a nevus, deformity, or any other sort of disability. Celebrate who you are and the wonderful things about your life. Maybe you are a talented artist, a business person, a mother, a father, a helpful friend, or a volunteer worker. No matter who you are or what you do, rejoice in it. Who could be more unique than Stephen Hawking, the English theoretical physicist, cosmologist, and author, who suffered from a rare early-onset amyotrophic lateral sclerosis (ALS), also known as Lou Gehrig's disease? In 1963, he contracted this motor neuron disease, and he was given two years to live. This disease gradually paralyzed him over the decades. He communicated using a single cheek muscle attached to a speech-generating device. What an inspiration he was and still is to others. However, he was a self-proclaimed atheist. The Bible says that when we die, we will be given new bodies, bodies that will never age or be subject to dying, because they will be like Christ's resurrection body. To me, it means that believers will receive new bodies, our perfect selves, that do not age, and we will enjoy eternal life in heaven. Mr. Hawking missed it, and that makes me very sad.

Living with a giant congenital nevus is beyond doubt a difficult situation, but *I have learned a lot of life lessons from it.* Here are a few of my life lessons:

* *It is possible to be happy even when you are different.* I find happiness every day simply by enjoying being alive and enjoying family and friends and the world around me; true happiness resides within my heart always. Especially when

I look at my granddaughters or even a bright blue sky with puffy white clouds, I look up and I think, *What a beautiful day the Lord has given us.*

* *Learn to not sweat the small stuff.* Live one day at a time, and live it to the fullest. This does not mean don't plan. I plan for everything.
* Many people don't like being different, and I am one of them; however, sometimes it's *an opportunity for amazing moments.* I have met a number of truly kind, helpful, and accepting people.
* *Have patience.* Patience has served me well through many difficult situations.
* *Have hope.* Hope can start out small, but as long as you hold onto it, it can grow like a snowball that you are rolling to create a huge snowman. Hope builds confidence that things will turn out fine, and when they do, it makes it easier to hope again!
* *Be persistent.* Persistence can be tough when the going gets rough, but keep it in mind that as long as you keep going, you'll eventually get to where you want to be.
* *Marry the right person.* I am extremely fortunate and truly blessed to have a wonderful husband at my side. Larry has helped me to overcome shyness and much insecurity.
* *Life is short. Embrace everything.* Those of us born with a giant congenital nevus live with the constant threat of developing melanoma. I live each day as though it was my last.
* *Doctors don't know everything.* Larry has always said this to me, and he is correct. They have remarkable skills that I fully respect, but they don't always have all the answers. Refer to patience a few lines back.
* *Have confidence.* The more confident you are will allow you to receive more positive responses in return. This is a tough one that took years to accomplish, but with Larry's help, I developed confidence. You have to practice.

* *Be grateful.* I don't focus on what other people have or what I don't have. I give thanks for the countless blessings that God has given to me.
* *Appreciate the little things.* Every little detail in life counts, fresh air, the way the dirt smells when I am planting flowers, sunshine, puffy white clouds, puppies, books, angels, and ice cream, especially ice cream!
* *Have true compassion for others.* Having compassion for others will help you form strong relationships, will help you to stop obsessing over yourself, and will make you feel less alone in the world.
* *Nobody is perfect.* We live in a society that glamorizes perfection. Models and celebrities are on the covers of magazines. They spend hours with professional makeup artists, *and* then pictures are photoshopped to perfection. The truth remains that there are no perfect people.

In the Beginning

She's got a pair of eyes
That are brighter than the summer sky
When you see them, you'll realize
Why I love my sweet Lorraine
—Nat King Cole, 1940

I (Lorraine Mary Clay) was born on March 30, 1960. They named me Lorraine because my mother and sister liked the song "Sweet Lorraine" that would play on the radio. I entered the world quietly by cesarean section with a giant congenital nevus which was almost black and covered most of my back and went all the way down my body, ending above my knees. The doctors told my mother that I would not live to see my fourth birthday. However, I am still here at age fifty-nine, happily married with a son and two beautiful granddaughters and a great career. How on earth did I make it, you may ask? Well, I am going to tell you. This is my story.

My mother, whose name was Rose Chabanik-Clay, never owned an automatic washing machine. She used what was then called a ringer washer, and it was hard work. She was born April 20, 1918, the sixth of ten children. She passed away in October of 1979 never knowing the convenience of an automatic washing machine or an automatic dryer. The only dryer she ever knew was the six rows of clothesline draped across our backyard. My dad made clothes *props* from tree branches to hold up the clothesline. 1979 was a time not really all that long ago in years but ancient history with the rapid social, religious, medical, economic, electronic, and environmental changes that have taken place since then.

We had a large backyard with a vegetable garden, a grape arbor, plum trees, and a peach tree. My dad made wine from the grapes, and my mother made grape preserves. She also made plum and peach preserves. In September, Mom would also can tomatoes from the garden. She must have canned at least fifty or more jars of tomatoes, and we enjoyed them all winter long. Our neighbor, Mr. Thatchen, had raspberry bushes that sometimes grew so large that they grew right into the back of our garden. I would sneak back there and eat raspberries right from the vine. You can't imagine how sweet and delicious they were, and I never got caught!

We had a swing in our yard that my dad made; three people could sit comfortably, and it had a brick patio under it and a real roof over it made from scrap lumber. It was not pretty, but we all loved it. My family was poor, but I never really knew it. My mother enriched my life in many ways. She called my nevus "my beauty mark." When I was very small, I thought that everybody had one!

Mom sat at the kitchen table every night first saying the rosary, and then she would listen to the radio station WMBS from Uniontown. The station had a talk show where you could call in and chat about anything. She would listen to it and play cards, solitaire. She would be there every night when I came home from dates. I still picture her sitting at the table in that little house in Shoaf every night when I go to sleep while I pray for her. Catholics pray for the dead; unfortunately, my list gets longer every year.

Sometimes, after school, in the evenings when mom was sitting on the couch, I would lay down and put my head in her lap, we would watch television together, and she would run her fingers through my hair. It's a perfect memory. It soothes me just to think about it although I miss her terribly.

One of my fondest memories as a child was waking up to the sound of her ringer washing machine on a summer morning. The house smelled so fresh like Tide and Clorox.

The breeze would billow the curtains as we did not have any sort of air conditioning, just screens in the windows. Everything my Mom did, she did with joy, even washing clothes, and she always had a beautiful smile for me. The old wringer washer was in our basement, and then she would carry the wet clothes up the stairs and outside to dry. In winter, there were clotheslines hung in our basement. That basement was a dismal place right out of a scary movie, but my mom made it inviting to me just because she was always down there working. I used to sit for hours on the stair steps and watch her make rugs on a loom. Thump, thump, screech, thump, thump, screech. It was really hard work, but there was an art to it that she loved. The handmade rugs were amazing, and people came from everywhere to buy them from her. She also made nut rolls (Kolachi) with her mother's recipe from Czechoslovakia for every holiday, not only for our family but also for her customers. She made nut, apricot, and poppy seed. They were made from scratch, and I remember huge pots of rising dough, and it made the house smell so wonderful. She placed the walnuts in a grinder, and I remember my dad would help her grind the nuts on a contraption that was screwed onto our kitchen table or the base of what people refer to now as a Hoosier. The typical Hoosier cabinet usually consisted of three parts. The one in our house had a base section and one large compartment with a slide out shelf and several drawers to one side. It sat on small casters. The top portion had smaller compartments with doors; it also had a sliding countertop. I can envision it sitting in the kitchen in my mind's eye right now.

Mom made extra money from selling her delicious nut rolls along with her rugs, and that is how she made ends meet and also how I got new school clothes and shoes. Every year, I received four dresses from the Spiegel Catalog and two pairs of shoes. The rest of my clothes were hand-me-downs from my cousins, and I loved getting them. My dad was a coal miner, but when the mine shut down, he worked for a company in Uniontown, Pennsylvania, which made parts for the coal mines that were still in operation. Some are still in operation today.

I was born with a giant nevus, but my mother never treated me differently than anyone else. She taught me that true beauty comes from within. She always encouraged me to do new things and to read and learn all that I could, but at the same time, she was very protective. I used to get to do fun things growing up in Shoaf; one of them was to go to the cemetery in Fairchance, and another was to get ice cream from the guy that drove the truck that played music. We called him the goody goody man, and I got a ten cent popsicle every day in the summer. The last but not the least was going to the dump with my dad. I loved finding books at the dump. I know what you are thinking, yuck. It was not a dump for food-type garbage or garbage at all. It was a dump that people brought their cast offs, furniture, appliances, books, broken toys, etc. One day, I pulled an entire geographical encyclopedia out of the rubble that was in a box. They were like brand new. My dad and I were the original pickers long before Mike and Frank thought up the hit History Channel TV show *American Pickers*. Dad would always find antiques and other miscellaneous treasures. About the cemetery, we always took Aunt Connie with us when we visited the cemetery. She would plant flowers on the graves, and I would help her, and then we would walk around and she would tell me about all of the people that were buried there. I was always intrigued with the section where the babies and children were buried. I loved going to the cemetery.

While living in Scotland, Larry (my husband) had the utmost patience with me as we toured the large historic cemeteries of Glasgow and Edinburgh. One of our first dates was visiting Larry's church, historic St. Peter's in Brownsville. The cemetery that surrounds Saint Peter's is magnificent. There are unique inscriptions on the aged headstones. The cemetery has been featured on *Ripley's Believe It or Not* as the only cemetery with heated graves. The boiler that heated the church was located in a separate building across the street, and the pipes running under the cemetery to the church created a significant enough amount of heat to even melt snow on several grave sites.

I grew up in a place that was out in the middle of nowhere at the foot of the Appalachian mountains in rural Pennsylvania called Shoaf. Shoaf is located about nine miles southwest of Uniontown between the little towns of Fairchance and Smithfield. I lived there until I was twenty-three years old. Shoaf was a small coal mining town also known as a company town or a coal mining patch. Long ago, there were about thirty-eight or more coal mining patch towns in Fayette County, and they all had their own baseball team, and my dad played for the Shoaf team. The Frick Coal Company opened the Shoaf mine in 1905. The houses were built in the same year. There were three hundred coke ovens built and burning by 1916 supported by the B&O railroad. Pittsburgh needed the coke to run the steel mills. The Shoaf mine closed in 1951, but the coke industry remained.

Shoaf was the name of the family that H. C. Frick bought the land from. They were called *company houses* because they were built and owned by the H. C. Frick *Company*. They were built duplex style, and each side of the duplex had two bedrooms upstairs, a kitchen and living room downstairs, and a basement. The bathroom was a portable copper tub usually placed in the kitchen to take baths, and trendy outhouses were all the rage usually having a wooden bench with two openings, a small one for the children and a larger one for the adults. Really fancy outhouses had three sizes. If it was winter and you didn't want to go outside, there was always a chamber pot. There were no bathrooms until the early 1950s, and my sister, Mary, remembers using the outhouse until she was in the fifth grade.

Every coal mining patch had a company store. Miners had credit for buying food, clothes, etc., at the company store, and this bill was deducted directly from their paychecks. Only men worked in the mines; women raised the family of four to eight or more children. Women worked at the company store, but once they got married, they had to quit. There was no social security back then; however, people raised large families, and the children were expected to take care of their elderly relatives, and they did.

Women baked and cooked on coal stoves in the summer as well as in winter. The coal stove also heated the house in wintry weather. Most of the coal was stored in the coal bin located next to the outhouse with a one-day supply of coal stored next to the stove. This required coal ash removal and disposable. In the winter, the beds where covered with goose feather-filled quilts to keep warm while sleeping.

When I was a little girl in the 1960s, we had a large coal bin under our front porch, and it fueled our coal furnace. I remember my mom and dad shoveling coal into the furnace day and night.

The H. C. Frick Coke Company awarded prizes for the best gardens and lawns at the various mining patches that they owned. The prizes were to encourage the miners and their families to take care of the yards and to raise the produce they needed. Kind of like our modern-day "Yard of the Month."

The town of Shoaf supported the local coal mine and the coke ovens that the mine supplied. Death was a constant factor as underground mining is inherently dangerous, and coal mining had the additional danger of methane gas, which can cause asphyxiation and explosions. Black lung disease caused by inhaling coal dust shortened the lives of many miners. The company (H. C. Frick) provided a company doctor for the coal miners and families. Babies were delivered at home by the company doctor or by midwives. My grandma Chabanik delivered lots of babies.

I actually lived just before the railroad tracks in Smiley. There wasn't a superintendent's house in Shoaf, but there was one in Smiley, and it was the nicest house for miles and was located just a short distance from the Shoaf company store. The coal mine at Shoaf closed in 1952, but the coke ovens burned day and night, with a few shutdowns for coal miner's strikes, etc., until 1972 when the Pennsylvania State Environmental Regulatory agency shut them down. I can picture them in my mind burning right now, that huge orange glow.

Sometimes, the smoke was so awful and thick on a summer's night that my mom would cart me off to spend the night at my friend Karen's house. The beehive coke ovens and our house were located in a bowl surrounded by steep hills. In the summer, coming down the hill, all you could see some nights was a ghostly white haze reminding me of Stephen King's *The Mist*. I could see monsters coming out of that eerie mist long before Stephen King wrote his book.

Company houses are unique in their development and role in immigrant housing. The coal company patch towns that are left are truly historical but also unique in the problems and issues that they are facing today. They are deteriorating and are faced with issues of being located out in the middle of nowhere, multiple ownership, and lack of initiative and funds for preservation. The wide range of coal patch towns existing in Fayette County is a unique trait of local culture. Lists of fourteen coal patches from 1880 to 1920 are being considered for preservation and rehabilitation with the most favorable locations being Shoaf and Lemont Furnace. Shoaf is currently listed on the National Register of Historic Places, but I don't know why. Anything of historical interest is covered with vegetation. You can't even see where the railroad tracks were.

Every spring, my mother would wash down the walls in our house, and she even washed the ceilings. The oily black sticky soot from the coke ovens covered everything. My mother died of colon cancer in October of 1979. Cancer or cancer-related illnesses affected five of her nine brothers and sisters, and many of our neighbors died from cancer. We lost my brother Joe at the age of fifty-seven from esophageal cancer in 2003. The number of cases of various cancers and birth defects is substantial in Shoaf and also in Fayette County as a whole. The town of Shoaf is very small, but cancers are numerous. Also, a child was born blind. I have a memory of two brothers that lived in Shoaf; they were a little younger than me, and they rode my school bus. They were born without the top layer of their skin, and their eyes were red, not the whites of their eyes but their actual eyes. From what I have researched, it could have been a type of harlequin ichthyosis. This condition literally occurs one in a million births. My personal opinion is that these conditions were a result of the radon gas from the mines and from inhaling "who knows what" they burned in the coke ovens. My father once came home from a walk and told my mother that he found large amounts of lead metal in the form of large pipes lying around behind one of the large ash dumps that were along the railroad tracks. He suspected that they were being disposed of by burning them in the coke ovens: of course this is only conjecture.

Our company house was two houses away from the railroad tracks. The coke ovens were just beyond the tracks. The roof on our house was the original slate roof from when it was built in 1905, and it leaked. When it rained, we had numerous buckets placed strategically around the two bedrooms upstairs. Every summer, my dad would climb up on that old slate roof and cover it with tar, and it would stop the leaking, at least for a while. The roofs on those old company houses were extremely high. I can remember him walking around on that roof like he was walking across the yard; he was fearless. In the winter, our windows froze solid all the way through. Waking up in the morning, I would watch my Jack and the Beanstalk curtains billow in and out from the wind coming through those old windows. My mom, dad, brother, and sister used an outhouse in the early days. Then later, they installed a fancy bathroom complete with toilet, sink, and shower. When I was little, we had a coal furnace which replaced the upstairs coal stove and fireplaces in 1949. Then my parents got really fancy in 1967 and had an oil furnace installed.

In 1905, when the house was built, there was a coal-burning fireplace in every room except the kitchen which had a coal stove. The original chimneys were filled in and closed by my dad. All except the one that serviced the coal furnace. My brother once told me that he remembers Dad pouring wet concrete down those chimneys. The fireplaces were covered over. You would never know that they actually existed.

It was a creepy old house. In the early 1900s and on in to the 1920s, the bereaved would lay their loved ones that had died right in the living room. Family and friends would come by to pay their respects. I'm guessing that many of them had died from mine accidents. We don't know anything about the people that lived in the house before my parents bought it; at least they never told any of us anything about them. Our next-door neighbor, Mr. Thatchen, was at least a hundred years old, at least to me when I was seven, he seemed at least one hundred years old. He spoke with a broken accent sounding a little like Bela Lugosi. In reality, he was probably in his late seventies or early eighties. Mr. Thatchen caught me playing in Mrs. Thatchen's rock garden one day (where I was not allowed to play) and asked me if I wanted to hear a story, and of course I said yes.

He whispers in his accent, "Do you hear the dogs outside howl late at night sometimes, little girl?"

I said, "Yes, I do, Mr. Thatchen, all the time (everybody had at least one or twenty dogs)."

He replies, "That is when the dead walk the earth to suck living souls deep into the bowels of hell."

As I went running and screaming to my mother, I made a mental note to never play in Mrs. Thatchen's garden ever again. I still ate raspberries from Mr. Thatchen's bushes but only the ones that grew into our garden of course.

The floor creaked in our house sometimes late at night, and I just knew that the undead were going to get me at any given moment. My mom slept with me until I fell asleep until I was twelve. My sister says that she truly believes that our house was haunted. I agree; I had a strange experience while living there but only once. It was autumn in the early 1970s, and my mother and I were watching *The Brady Bunch* in the dark on our black and white television with its *snowy* picture in our living room. My dad was outside relaxing on the swing. Mom and I heard a very loud thud in the little hall connecting the kitchen to the living room. So I turned on the light and went to investigate. I found our sugar jar standing upright on the floor in the hallway. It traveled eight feet from the kitchen to the hallway without spilling one grain of sugar. We were astounded. I had a reoccurring dream that the house was burning down as far back as I can remember. I had that dream at least once or twice a year. In 1986, long after we had moved and sold the house, it burned down to the ground.

If my mom could come and visit me today, she would be in awe at how wonderfully different my current house is to the Shoaf house that she and my dad raised three children in. Larry and I had our house built in 2012. It's exceedingly different from the little house in Shoaf. Also, cell phones today are actually tiny computers, and GPS for the car is similar as the artificial intelligence tells you where to turn and how long the trip will take, and it will warn you of heavy traffic. Mom would be in total amazement of these simple items. We did not have a telephone in our house until I was about five years old, and back then, mostly everyone had a party line. That meant that up to three or four families shared the line.

If you picked up the phone to use it and heard someone talking, you had to hang up and wait until they were finished. When I was about nine or ten, we got a private line. That made us high society in Shoaf as no one else had a private line.

Between 1815 and 1915, some thirty million Europeans arrived in the United States, and for many, it was a long and difficult journey. It was not the best of times, but most families came to America before 1914 and missed living in Europe during World War I and World War II. My grandparents (Steve Joseph and Konstantina Catherine Chabanik) on my mother's side were two of them. They came to the United States from Czechoslovakia around 1906. My grandfather went to work in the coal mine at Shoaf. They did not live in a company house; however, they did live in the middle of the patch known as Smiley. It was a very tiny house on about a half-acre of land. My grandfather added a second floor to the tiny house because they needed the room to raise ten children, but guess what, it was still tiny with three bedrooms. But to me, it was like a mansion sitting among all of the company houses. I remember a white picket fence all the way around it, and there was a barn, outhouse, chicken coop, and some other buildings.

Their house was a stone's throw from the house that I grew up in. I remember my grandpap, he died when I was six, but I have very fond memories of him. Apparently, I was a rambunctious child (actually I was spoiled and defiant) who would steal every chance I could to get away from my mother and *run up the hill* to Grandpap's house. So Mom simply took a dog collar and tied me to the clothesline with a small light chain by my ankle.

Grandpap walked down to visit us one day and had a fit in broken English. *Rosie, why for you tie her like dog to the clothesline?* And then the rest was in loud Slovak. So I was never tied to the clothesline again. Grandma Chabanik died in 1957 before I was born. I am the youngest of the Chabanik grandchildren, and there are *a lot* of us. Not to mention hundreds of cousins, none of them have a nevus that I know of.

Living with a giant birthmark is a bit like being tied up. We want to look and be just like everyone else, and we don't want the risk of melanoma. But we *are* different, and we *don't* look like everyone else plus we *do* live with the risk of cancer. These factors hold us back from being who we truly are and who we truly want to be, if we let them. They influence our relationships, activities, behaviors, and interactions. I learned to pray a lot, and as an adult, I do breathe prayers throughout the day. It helps a great deal.

I have had my share of bad days and feeling sorry for myself. I remember looking out of my bedroom window at the rain falling down in winter. It was just a few degrees short of being snow on those cold bleak rainy days. I would study the company houses across the street, and if I looked sideways out of the corner of the window on the right, I could see up to Grandpap's house. One day, I looked down at a doll that I was holding. She had a crack in her plastic leg, but I loved her anyway. I felt a lot like my doll that day. Because of my birthmark, I suffered with a profoundly indescribable feeling of loneliness because I thought that no one in the whole wide world was like me, and I was afraid. Not all of the time, but sometimes I had my moments. It made me suffer from social anxiety. At school, I never looked at anybody while walking through the halls. This made people think that I was a snob. Don't get me wrong, I had a ton of friends; however, I could have had tons more if I had been more confident.

I remember walking with my mother along the road that led *up the hill* to my grandparent's house to visit my grandfather and my Aunt Connie who lived with him. We went almost every day. When I was really little, Mom would dress me in playsuits, and my birthmark would show. One of the neighbors looked at me and then at my mom with a woeful expression on her face and said, "Well, at least she has a pretty face." Other people would say, "Thank goodness her face is not marked." I was puzzled by their comments. Now at age fifty-nine (as I write this), I know of many fellow nevus wearers that have a facial nevus, and I find them beautiful. I admire their courage and strength in a world constantly absorbed in flawless beauty. *Flawless beauty is not genuine beauty.*

My father's family (Clay) came here from I believe what was called Austria at the time. Last week, I knew virtually nothing about my dad's family; however, while writing this book, I found myself wanting to research the Clay side of my family who also lived in a coal mining patch called Continental Number 2. What I found was fascinating, at least to me!

My dad's parents came to this country around 1887. They were Jacob and Katharine Clay. Grandmother went by the name Katie as it is listed that way in the 1900 census. They married in 1898. They went on to have eight children, my father, Joseph G. Clay being the youngest. My father was born December 12, and Katie Clay, his mother, passed away in January. He felt guilty for her death his entire life. The 1920 census has my dad as being three years old and living in house number 148 only it was not in Continental, it was in another coal mining patch called Orient, Pennsylvania. All of the Clay children were born in Orient, Pennsylvania.

The 1940 US Census lists my father Joseph G. Clay and lists both of his parent's birthplaces as Hungary. So then I thought that the Clays were Hungarian. However, thanks to the power of the Internet and my friends on Facebook, I have the following information. "Back then, it was considered the Austrian-Hungarian Empire which encompassed the entire area of Czechoslovakia, Hungary, Austria, Poland, and Yugoslavia from 1869 to 1918, and our ancestors were under its rule even though we were Slovaks from Slovakia. That is probably why our ancestors came to America. And our little patch area of western Pennsylvania was the gathering point of many of these Slovaks. Slovaks were part of the second major wave of immigration to the United States (the first wave was from Ireland and Germany). Targets of major discrimination and xenophobia (an intense fear or dislike of foreign people, their customs, and culture) as unionization of industry began in the United States."

The 1940 census lists my dad as being twenty-two years old and living in house number 75 in Continental Number 2. It lists my dad as working in a coke yard as a laborer and making $200 (guessing that was a month), that his highest grade completed in school was eighth, it lists him as being single, and that his native language was Slovak. My mom and dad were married in October of 1940. I know nothing about how they met, what kinds of dates they went on, or how we ended up living in Shoaf. My sister, Mary, thinks that when they were first married, they lived with family. As with my mother's side of the family, none of my many cousins and relatives on the Clay side has a nevus that I know of.

My mom was forty-two years old when she had me. My big sister, Mary Catherine, was almost eighteen, and my big brother, Joe, was sixteen, so I was quite a surprise. It was a difficult birth, and I was born just before midnight. My sister remembers it as after midnight, so who really knows, it may have been March 31.

I do not know (medically) very much about myself as a newborn, toddler, or young child, but I bet that it involved a lot of needles. I have a severe phobia of needles. This also pertains to sewing needles. It takes me three hours to put a hem in a skirt, so most of the time, I send garments to a seamstress. I can, however, remember going off to a doctor in Fairchance to have inoculations needed to enter school. It was horrifying for me, and from what I remember, I was carried in and chased around the room, when caught, the male doctor would hold me down while his wife, the nurse, gave me the huge needle, and when you are five years old, the needle is five miles long. They would always prepare it in front of me, and the part where they squirt liquid pain out of the top of the five mile long needle is making me nauseous right now just to remember it. My family physician medicates me when I have to go for procedures or blood tests or any needle type tests. It's embarrassing. I recently read that physicians are doing studies on needle phobic people (both children and adults) across the nation. I have not done this yet, but if you are needle phobic, ask your doctor for EMLA numbing cream. It also dilates your veins. I'm getting lightheaded just writing this.

When I was born, my Aunt Connie Chabanik (my mother's sister who lived just "up the hill" in my grandparent's house) stayed with us during the day because my mother needed help. She is the only Chabanik sibling that never married. But she was sweet and kind, and she was everybody's mother, and she was skilled at cooking and baking and apparently taking care of infants. I have a photo of me as a newborn lying on a soft fluffy pillow, and Aunt Connie is in the picture. My nevus covers most of my back. Mom told me that it was dark when I was born, and it had black areas that would sometimes bleed. It became lighter as I grew and did not bleed anymore. I have never had any seizures.

My mother taught me how to pray, and as far back as I can remember, she would sit on my bed with me every night, and we would pray. First was the Lord's Prayer, then Hail Mary, and, last, The Glory Be, and then we would say our personal prayers which started with, "Please, Lord, take Lori's birthmark away," and then several other prayers and always ended with, "and please, Lord, keep Sonny" (meaning my brother Joe) "out of the war" (Vietnam). My brother's unit in the Marine Corp was never called to Vietnam, but I still have my birthmark. It's OK! I would rather keep my nevus than see my brother go to that terrible war that we watched on the six o'clock news every night. Mom said that if I prayed hard enough, Jesus would make my birthmark go away just like he made the blind man see. So I prayed really hard. What Mom didn't realize was that God intended for me to keep my birthmark. Aunt Connie explained it to me one day while I was at her house (up the hill), helping her water her flowers.

I said, "Aunt Connie, no matter how hard I pray, Jesus doesn't seem to hear me."

She said, "What are you praying about?"

I answered, "I'm asking for my birthmark to go away. Mom says that if I really believe and pray hard enough, Jesus will take it away just like he fixed the blind man's eyes so that he could see."

Aunt Connie knelt down to me, I must have been about nine years old, and she said, "Lori, Jesus could take your birthmark away, but I don't think that he is going too because he made you a very special person, and I think that he wants for you to keep it."

From then on, I knew it would never go away; however, ever year, it continues to get lighter and lighter.

I asked my mother one day not to long after I had my discussion with Aunt Connie. "Mom, how do we know that God is real?"

She answered, "God is real because he gave me your sister, your brother, and you." Then she said, "Look up at the sky" (as we were outside, I was watching her hang clothes on the clothesline), and I did. "Do you see how blue the sky is and the beautiful white fluffy clouds? All of this came from God. The flowers came from him and the trees and the rainbows. Even the kind things that people say to us comes from God. How else could they possibly exist?"

I never questioned the existence of God after that wonderful explanation.

I think that positive attitudes in life are partly learned behavior. My positive attitude came from my family especially my mother who I was always with night and day. She never stopped encouraging me. I never saw her cry although I know she must have. She was very strong, and I wanted to be just like her. Growing up, I always tried to focus on what was going right instead of what was going wrong. It has been said that positive people raise positive children, and negative people raise negative children. Was my home life always ideal, no it was not, but hard times will make you appreciate the good parts of your life and will make you even more grateful for what you have.

My brother, Joseph G. Clay Jr., was sixteen when I was born. I don't remember much about him living at home. However, I do remember that he walked around in his underwear and Mom would tell him to put clothes on. I remember him coming back from boot camp when he joined the marines. He brought me a little silver cross necklace. I remember that he was a phenomenal big brother, the best brother ever. Mom would let me stay up late on Saturday nights so that when he got back from a date, we could watch *Chiller Theater with Bill Cardille* (Chilly Billy) together. He would eat bottles of baby aspirin as we watched, the little pink ones, because he liked the way they tasted (Mom would get mad). I usually fell asleep not long after it started, and I'm guessing that he carried me up the stairs and put me to bed. He loved to hunt and fish. Rabbit, pheasant, and venison were weekly meals at our house, and they were delectable; rabbit was my favorite. I have not eaten rabbit in over thirty-six years. My brother would get a buck season hunting license and bring home a deer, he would get a doe season hunting license and bring home another deer, and *then* he would get a West Virginia hunting license for buck season and usually brought home a deer. He would then get a doe season license for West Virginia and usually bring home a deer. We ate a lot of deer (venison). My brother loved deer hunting so much that he would drive up into the mountains to buy fox pee from a fox pee breeder. He would then cover himself in fox pee so the deer would not smell him. I went with him a couple of times, and let me tell you, fox pee smells really dreadful, especially on a huge fox pee farm.

Ever since I was really little, I loved music. My earliest memory of music was the little record player I had and my brother Joe buying me Beatles albums and 45s. By age six, I knew every word of every Beatle song. I still do (pre-Sergeant Pepper). Mom made me sing for everyone that visited our house because they didn't believe her when she told them I could sing every word. Then I had to recite nursery rhymes that she and my sister taught me when I was three. Now I have a vast collection of music on this tiny little thing called an iPod. What would my mother think of this i-pod thing? I still stare in wonder at this gadget.

Joe married Carole in 1967, and I was a flower girl in their wedding (I was seven). I was terrified to walk down that l-o-n-g aisle at the church. When you are seven, everything is super gigantic. When you are a seven-year-old with a birthmark that people stare at, people looking at you is uncomfortable, even when your birthmark is hidden. When it was my turn to walk down the aisle, I was terrified and turned around, but my savior that day was Suzie, the "big girl" flower girl. I think she was around twelve. Suzie told me, "Lori, don't be afraid. I will walk with you. We will do it together. Let's go." And she smiled at me. So down the aisle we went with cameras flashing and the ohhhs and ahhhs of how cute we were. So crisis averted, I made it to the altar and through the rest of the ceremony.

My brother's death at age fifty-seven due to esophageal cancer was devastating for everyone that knew him, but it was especially devastating to his wife, his four children, his grandchildren, his sisters, his nieces and nephews, and his in-laws. He knew a lot of people, and everyone loved him. I remember the line to get into the funeral home was wrapped all the way down the street and around the corner. It's quite true that he never knew a stranger. He was extremely friendly, helpful, and someone you could always count on, and he had an amazing sense of humor and could really tell a story (when I was sad, he always made me laugh). He was my mother's favorite child! She loved all three of us, but she *beamed* when he entered the room. I smile as I write this because it is so true.

I remember being in the car with him driving somewhere on my thirteenth birthday.

Joe said to me, "Lori, you are entering the absolute best years of your life. Enjoy every day because your teenage years fly by way to fast." He was right. He taught me how to drive a car and then took me for my driver's test. *He knew the policeman*, so I passed! He taught me how to catch night crawlers (big fat worms) so that he could use them fishing. There was quite a technique to it. This is how we did it in Pennsylvania. Wait until it is almost dark and water the lawn. Then when it is dark, you take a flashlight and step very softly looking through the grass for big fat worms, they stick their heads out, then swoosh (you have to be really fast), you grab one and pull it out and throw it in a bucket. It was so cool because some worms were up to twelve inches long. He bought me my first puppy. He gave me rides to high school football games and a myriad of other places.

My brother was a magnificent father, grandfather, and brother. He was a coal miner and lived at the foot of the mountains in rural Pennsylvania. He worked really hard. He loved his family. He had a lot of talents such as cooking, gardening, and taxidermy. He had huge vegetable gardens with tomatoes, peppers, onions, corn, potatoes, etc. He loved being a taxidermist, and it went right along with his hunting skills. Taxidermy is the art of preparing, stuffing, and mounting the skins of animals for display (e.g., as for hunting trophies) for himself personally and also for many others. He also raised turkeys.

Joe and Carole had four children. Antoinette Jo (Toni) was the firstborn in 1968, then came Todd Joseph, then Thomasine Joy (Tommye), and then as a big surprise, they had Teri Lynn in 1981. She and my Michael were born a month apart. When I was growing up and lived in Shoaf, my brother and his family lived only a few minutes away, so we saw them almost every day. I remember my nephew and nieces since the day they were born, but I am sure they don't have as many memories of me because Larry and I moved away from Pennsylvania in 1983. It was fun to have them living nearby, and I was always especially close with Toni; she was my little shadow. Toni saw my birthmark plenty of times but never really noticed it. They are all grown with families of their own. I haven't seen them in years but still love them all very much. Todd has a little boy named Joseph after my brother. My sister Mary says that little Joseph looks exactly the same as my bother did as his age. I know that my brother can see us from heaven and is beaming with joy at his beautiful grandchildren. I am pretty sure that the Lord our God has made him an official greeter at the pearly gates. I can't think of a better angel station post than that for him, and when I leave this world someday, whether it is tomorrow or when I'm ninety-nine, I am positive that he will be one of the first there to greet me probably with our mother.

School Days, Friends, and Fun

Value generosity, humility, goodness, kindness, and love

There were no other children to play with where I lived. I used to watch Miss Jan on Romper Room and was so excited at the thought of going to school. I did not go to kindergarten because in the early 1960s, parents had to provide transportation. I looked forward to first grade like it was going to be Christmas. I was so excited to ride on the bus and go to school with the big kids.

The day finally arrived. I had a brand new dress and fancy shoes and lunch money! I rode the great big orange bus to D. Ferd Swaney Elementary School, September of 1966. My bus stop was the first stop, so I got to choose any seat that I wanted. I sat up front. It was a long bus ride all through the windy rural roads that didn't even have names back then. The ride was about forty-five minutes. When I got to school, I went to Mrs. Clark's room. But where were the toys? Romper room had toys! Mrs. Clark was old and impatient and just plain mean. Mrs. Clark yelled, "Little girl, put down the lid of your desk." I looked across the aisle at a little girl with the bluest eyes I had ever seen. She had her sweater in her mouth, and much like the rest of us, she was scared! She was startled and put down the lid of her desk really quick. Her name was Cindy, and she had a tiny little brown beauty mark on the side of her face. Cindy and I became fast friends. We are friends to this day.

The playground was an enchanting place. There were swings and a slide and little metal animals on big springs that the student could rock back and forth. They were brightly colored, and everybody wanted to ride them especially me! By the time I got out onto the playground, the rocking animals were already being rocked on.

But one day, I was able to get to ride the bright little horse; it was fantastic. Rock, rock, rock, what great fun it was, and then I noticed some of the other little girls staring at me. In the 1960s, when little girls went to school, they wore dresses and socks. Apparently, my birthmark was showing just above my knee. Then it happened.

"Hey, why are your legs dirty? Dirty legs, dirty legs."

I was shattered. "My legs aren't dirty. I have a birthmark" (still smiling).

Then came, "Don't play with *her*. Eww, yuck, she has dirty legs." And they all ran away.

But know what, Cindy did not run away. She said, "Let's be friends." And we are until this very day although we live very far apart. This was my introduction into the first grade and the real world of how cruel children (and people in general) can be to one another. That was the moment that I lost a lot of self-esteem and became a very shy little girl that sometimes acted out with odd behavior.

I went home that day with mixed emotions and told my mom all about it. She bought me tights and pettipants! Pettipants were like a petticoat, only with pants to wear under dresses. They were awesome. She told me not to worry about the children calling me names and taught me the sticks and stones saying. She said the other children just didn't know how wonderful I was because they didn't know me yet. My mother was an amazing, loving person.

My sister, Mary Katherine, is just the best sister that anyone could ever imagine. She was named for our Aunt Mary Katherine who was my mother's eldest sister. She has been there for me my entire life. She is *awesome*. I am so very blessed to have her in my life, my second mommy. When I was little, she would send me surprise boxes of tights that she bought at the hosiery factory in Asheboro, North Carolina, where she and her husband, Richard, still reside. They came in every color, red, blue, black, brown, and white, and I loved them. You could not see my birthmark through them. Back in the late 1960s early 1970s, tops for girls (similar to T-shirts) were made that snapped at the crotch. You wore them with jeans and didn't have to worry about your tucked-in shirt coming undone. They looked very smooth and polished, and I liked them a lot. Mary sent me four of them, and one was white. It was so pretty, but it was made of a thinner material, and you could see my birthmark on my back right through it and my bra in the front (which was even worse). So Mom and Aunt Connie went to work. My mom could sew, but Aunt Connie could s-e-w! She made from a white T-shirt the perfect cutouts and sewed them into my top. It was flawless. I would have worn it every day if mom would have allowed it.

Remember the doll back in the 1960s, Beautiful Crissy with Hair that Grows? I got one for Christmas. I loved that doll. During a childhood illness, can't remember which one, but it was either chicken pox or German measles, Aunt Connie made my Beautiful Crissy doll clothes to cheer me up. It took my breath away. It was spectacular, dresses and slacks and skirts and tops, and she even made hats complete with a hat pin. Then she made a box that resembled a closet with drawers and everything, and she decorated that box with wallpaper. I am very blessed to have had so many wonderful women in my life.

Speaking of measles, I had every childhood illness you can think of. I had the vaccines but got sick anyway. I had whooping cough, mumps, three types of measles, and chicken pox. My mother nursed me through all of them. In the first grade, I missed around eighty days of school. I don't know how I passed to the second grade, but I did. Mom made sure I had my lessons at home. The reason I am writing about this is because when I had measles and chicken pox, *none of the bumps appeared on my nevus-related skin.* So that meant that I had double bumps everywhere else including the whites of my eyes.

My Aunt Irene used to come from Cleveland, Ohio, to Aunt Connie's house just about every summer. She and Uncle Joe had five children, and they would make the trip in what was to me a great big station wagon. One summer, when I was about seven years old, she put up a swimming pool which was to me a great big swimming pool. I got to go swimming! I was there every day in my shorts and tank top. My cousin, Monica, was in charge of me not drowning, and she did a pretty good job. I had the time of my life that summer.

Aunt Irene was fun. Another summer, she took all of us to the mountains. At first, I was not allowed to go, but I cried and Aunt Irene promised to watch me very closely. It went like this. "Rosie, let Lorraine" (which is me, my birth name is Lorraine) "come with us to the mountains."

Mom said, "No, she can't go."

"Why not?"

"Irene, she will get poison on her birthmark. She may fall down a hillside and never been seen again. There is water, and she could drown, she may get a spider bite, she may get a snake bite, she's delicate, and there are copperheads in those mountains. Irene, anything could happen, so no, she can't go."

I was crying, wailing, and begging "*Please* let me go, Mommy, *please*. I promise I won't get hurt. I promise I'll be careful and stay by Aunt Irene and Aunt Connie."

Aunt Irene looked my mother square in the eye and said, "Rosie, I will have her by my side every minute. She will be fine."

So my mom let me go. As soon as we arrived at that glorious destination, Aunt Irene said, "Kids, go and play, have fun, and watch out for Lorraine."

My cousins took off in every direction, and I followed in a triumphant glorious pace hardly keeping up because I was the youngest. We climbed hills in the weeds, we walked through streams, we saw deer, we saw rabbits and all kinds of birds, and we found mysterious dwellings which I later learned were used by the boy scouts. And what I remember the most was how beautiful it was there with all the trees, how beautiful nature was, and how fresh everything smelled. We had a magnificent day which ended with a gigantic picnic feast that I remember to this day because the Chabaniks never did anything small when it came to food (a tradition carried on by my sister, Mary, and many other Chabanik family members). It was one of the best days of my entire life. I did not know how special growing up at the foot of that huge mountain was until I became an adult and moved away. Part of my heart and my childhood will always be there.

In the third grade, in Mrs. Hiscar's class, I met my friend, Karen. She, just like my friend Cindy, was Catholic. So not only did

I see them in school, we also went to Catechism together on Saturday mornings at Saint Cyril and Methodius Roman Catholic Church in Fairchance. Karen and I rode the same bus, and she invited me to her house to spend the rest of the Saturday with her and her parents. I talked to my mom about it, and she called to speak to them and then said that it would be fine. This was the start of a wonderful friendship. Her grandparents lived with Karen and her parents. They were extremely kind people and were very nice to me. Karen's grandma made the most delicious food. After spending a few Saturdays there, I started calling her grandma too.

I thought that they were absolutely very wealthy and lived in a mansion. They had a lovely house with a formal living room and also a family room where we would watch *American Bandstand*. They had *two* bathrooms; one of the bathrooms had a tub in it which I *loved*, and when I was allowed to stay overnight, I loved soaking in that tub. Karen's room was just the perfect little girl's room with beautiful sheets and a comforter and beautiful dolls everywhere and a full basement filled with games and toys. They took me on my first trip to Kennywood Park which is an amusement park in Pittsburgh (the roller coaster capital of the world), Idelwild Park, Story Book Forest, and lots of other places.

We had a lot of fun, but the most fun was the summer that Karen got a swimming pool. I think we were about ten or eleven years old. So my mom explained to Karen and her family about my birthmark. They were very kind loving people and accepted me totally and let me know that I should not be ashamed about my birthmark. I have many happy memories of them; they were very understanding, and I actually wore one of Karen's bathing suits. We would spend entire days in the pool that summer. It was so much fun. Karen was my maid of honor when Larry and I married. I have not seen her in over twenty years, but we do communicate through Facebook.

Shady Grove Park

Ooh, I go swimming, swimming in the water
Swimming in the river, swimming in the sea
I go swimming
I go swimming, swimming in the water
Swimming in the pool, swimming is cool
I go swimming.

—Peter Gabriel, 1983

I never in my life so far have ever owned a real bathing suit, but one day, when I was about eight years old, I inherited one from somebody. I can't remember who it was, but I loved getting bags of hand-me-downs from my many cousins. One time, there was the cutest bathing suit just my size, and the bottom of it was like a little skirt. I put it on with a T-shirt on top, as it was cut very low in the back, and I pranced around the house in it all day long. There was a local public swimming pool named Shady Grove Park. I wanted to go swimming so badly, but I was afraid. I used to dream about how fun it would be to splash around in the water and learn to swim. I had such fun in Aunt Irene's pool, and I thought that I would never get to go to a pool ever again. When I got that bathing suit, I asked my mom if she would let me go swimming at Shady Grove with my brother, Joe, and his wife, Carole. They used to go swimming there every now and then. Mom was worried about it but thought it may be fun for me and asked my brother to take me there and he agreed. I was so excited but terrified at the same time.

When we got there, I noticed that the pool was huge; one side was the deep end for grownups, and the other was shallow for children. I went over to the children's section, but I was afraid. When I protested, the adults said, "It's OK. We will be right over here. Just play with the kids." So I took off the towel I had wrapped around my waist and climbed down the little steps into the pool. Right away, all eyes were on me, and I noticed that several parent's promptly took their children out of the pool and left. So I stood in the corner of the pool and watched everyone on the "big people" side. I was mortified, and I was planning on standing there all day in the water so that no one would see my birthmark and get scared away. After a little while that seemed like an eternity, I did not cry, but I wanted to. Just then, a large family that had just moved into a big empty house in the big city of Smiley showed up. We all knew each other and rode the same school bus. They did not care about my birthmark at all, and we walked around the pool in circles, talking, laughing, and playing in the water. We had the entire children's section of the pool for most of the afternoon that day, and when it was time to go, I was actually sad to leave the public pool. I, however, never went back. I'm kind of glad that the adults that gave me a ride to Shady Grove left me by myself on the kiddies' side. It was character building, and it was another life lesson. Someone once said that the struggle you are in today is developing the strength you need for tomorrow. I love that saying.

North Carolina

In my mind I'm goin' to Carolina
Can't you see the sunshine
Can't you just feel the moonshine
Ain't it just like a friend of mine
To hit me from behind
Yes, I'm goin' to Carolina in my mind.

—James Taylor, 1970

While growing up, I spent many summers at my sister's house in North Carolina. My sister, Mary Katherine Clay-Balog; her husband, Richard; and my niece and nephew, Tanya and Tarus, would usually drive up to Pennsylvania for the Fourth of July. I would drive back to North Carolina with them, and then they would bring me back home at the end of the summer until I was old enough to fly on an airplane by myself. I think that the first time I flew on my own was when I was eleven years old. They were the best summers of my life. I was nine the first time I visited North Carolina. I thought that they were fabulously wealthy. They had a brand new house built in 1966. It's a sprawling brick ranch with four bedrooms and three bathrooms and a full basement, and the price tag in 1966 was a whopping $21,000. It was in a real neighborhood with great neighbors, and *all* the kids had *bikes*, so therefore, to me, all of the neighbors were fabulously wealthy too. They still live in that same house, and it is still paradise to me. Larry and I try to visit at least once or twice a year. It's one of the few places I totally relax.

My sister is the nicest, sweetest, most thoughtful, loving, accepting person that I have ever known. I have never heard her say a curse word. She won't even kill a bug. She catches a house spider in a jar and lets it go outside. She loves animals and once took in a stray cat; I think his name was Tom (tomcat). Tom the cat had a sinus condition, so she took him to the vet to get him medicine so that he would stop sneezing. Mary hands out mountains of candy at Halloween. She feeds the birds and the squirrels, chipmunks, and the occasional raccoon everyday summer and winter. Richard now helps her with that since they are both retired. My brother-in-law, Richard, will give you the shirt off his back in an instant if you need one. Whenever the going gets tough, Mary and Rich are always there for us and for everyone they know and sometimes people that they don't know!

I am in awe of my sister's talents. She's smart, she's gracious, she's a great cook, she can bake like no one else, she is a great gardener, she sews, she is creative, and she is a magnificent mother, grandmother, and big sister. Mary is artistic, and she can wrap a present that is so truly beautiful you don't want to unwrap it. She should have been a surgical nurse because she loves to watch surgeries on television and once asked her surgeon if she could stay awake to watch him perform an arthroscopic procedure on her knee. I have never heard her utter one bad thing about anyone; she has extreme patience and just loves everybody. I wish that I could be more like her.

My brother-in-law, Richard, is a family man, hardworking, kind, loving, and always willing to help people. He is an amazing role model to his entire family. Richard and my husband, Larry, are two peas in a pod.

They love the world of finance and often have long discussions about this stock or that company, and they like the same types of movies. They never run out of things to talk about. When I was really little, I remember Richard coming to our house in Shoaf, and he would always carry a brown briefcase. He would sit down in the living room and read the *Wall Street Journal*. Then he would look over important papers from said briefcase. He taught me to save money. I always had a piggy bank, and I would save pennies, nickels, dimes, and quarters in it. Then when he would come to visit in the summer, he would count all of the change and roll it into paper rolls to take to the bank. I was six years old the first time we went to the bank. The teller was very high up in the air, a skyscraper to me; he picked me up so that I could see what was going on. He and Mary opened a savings account for me, and we deposited the money. He taught me a very valuable lesson about saving money, and it stayed with me my whole life. It's amazing how children (grownups too) will respond when they know that someone is rooting for them, encouraging them, and cheering them on. Mary and Rich were my biggest cheerleaders.

I remember on my first visit to North Carolina that there was a swing set in the backyard, and in a flash, I was on it. Five minutes later, six kids showed up to play with me, sheer nirvana.

In North Carolina, through the years, I learned to ride a bike, swim, bait a hook, catch a fish, and walk with no shoes on *everywhere,* I learned independence, I learned to follow rules, I learned that my sister could hold a two-year-old Tanya Balog, cook dinner, and ice homemade cupcakes at the same time, I learned about Charlie Chips (potato chips), I learned that I could never beat my three year old nephew Tarus at a board game, I discovered Cheerwine soda pop, I watched *Soul Train* for the first time (it came on right after *American Bandstand*), my first trip to a planetarium, I had my first fried okra (*yum*), my first ice cream supper at the church they attend, my first time going to a Presbyterian church, my first time visiting a veterinary clinic when we had to take a not feeling well Frisky the cat, and my first boat ride and on and on, it was just the best. There were *no birthmarks* in North Carolina.

Asheboro, North Carolina, had a fantastic public pool. The city had the big pool, and the city also had a smaller children's pool totally separate from the big pool. One summer, Mary bought me a one-piece short set that had a little cut out at the tummy. It was so cute, and I swam in that outfit all summer. When I was in the water, you could still see my birthmark, but it was OK because I was having so much fun I really didn't care. None of the other children seemed to notice. My nephew, Tarus, was four, my niece, Tanya, was three, and I was ten. We went to the kiddie pool *every day*! I learned to hold my breath and swim under water there, and I came back to Pennsylvania with two oval tan marks on my tummy. Best summer ever.

We usually had some sort of fun trip to go on each summer. We went to visit The Buffalo Ranch, The Land of Oz, Tweetsie Railroad, The Biltmore House, The Cherokee Indian Reservation, Carowinds, Myrtle Beach, White Lake, Old Salem, The North Carolina Zoo, The Planetarium in Raleigh, and so many other places. My summers were so much fun, and I wore Bermuda shorts with reckless abandon.

The first time I saw the ocean was a trip to Myrtle Beach, South Carolina. I wore my one-piece short set swimsuit outfit. In years to come, Mary and Rich bought me a pink bicycle with butterfly handlebars and a banana seat and brought it from North Carolina to Pennsylvania for me. I rode it every day all day long for years and years. Gosh, I loved that bike. My birthmark would sometimes show when I rode it, but I didn't care at all. Mary and Rich also allowed me to bring a puppy home to Pennsylvania one year. The car trip back then was around nine hours, and the puppy pooped on me and in the car. Tarus had a weak stomach so he threw up, luckily not on me.

My nephew, Tarus Paul Balog, was my parent's very first grand-child. There was much celebration the evening that we got the phone call. "Mary had the baby. It's a boy. Mom and baby doing well." My dad was thrilled that it was a boy. Mom was also thrilled to be a grandma, and she was also thrilled that his middle name was Paul. She announced to everyone she knew and even to those that she did not know that she was a grandma and the baby's name was Tarus *Paul*. She would say, "He is named after the pope, you know." I became an auntie at the age of six, actually five because he was born in January, and March of that year 1966, I turned six. At present day, Tarus and his wife, Andrea, live near Raleigh, North Carolina, out in the country on twenty-four acres. They have a beautiful house, horses, hens, and a huge garden.

Then a year later along came Tanya Renee Balog, she was a beautiful baby with curly hair and big blue eyes, and I was thrilled that she was a girl. In the 1980s, she won the Miss Randolph County Pageant. She is beautiful inside and out, and she is more of a little sister to me than my niece. She is now Tanya Wilson and lives near Charlotte, North Carolina, with husband, Jurgen, and twins, Taylor

Richard and Elsa Catherine, who at the time of this writing are sixteen. They are my favorite teenagers, and we love them very much.

Visiting North Carolina to me was heaven, but I did miss my mom a lot. When I came back to Pennsylvania, I was so glad to see her. I would arrive back usually a few days before the much dreaded school year began. I always hated school. I was an extremely good student. I just hated school. Children are cruel and so are teachers. In fifth grade, when we had to stand up and say what we did during the summer, the teacher did not believe me. I told the class about my sister and the fun things we did and my ride on the jet airplane back to the Pittsburgh airport.

My teacher said, "Young lady, I hope that you don't expect the class to believe that you actually flew on an airplane." She really did not believe me, but most of the children did. I got asked a lot of questions at recess about flying on an airplane.

Junior and Senior High School

Cast all your anxiety on Him.

—Peter 5:7

When I was in the seventh grade, there was an evil teacher. Her name was Mrs. Otto, and I will never forget her because she scared me so badly I would tremble. She was a ghastly, mean, horrible old woman, and everyone including the other teachers feared her. I had her for seventh bell which was the last bell (class) of the day. It made for a very long anxiety-filled day. All she did was scream and punish. This was back in the early 1970s when corporal punishment was allowed. She had a wooden paddle and used it frequently. To add to the horror, she would sometimes just randomly pick kids out and paddle them for no particular reason. My mom, since my first day of school in the first grade, had a note inserted in my file. *My child has a large birthmark and cannot under any circumstances be paddled.*

One day, at seventh bell, all the girls that were trying out for cheerleader got to go to tryouts. The rest of us, the square pegs, got to stay in Mrs. Otto's class. There were no boys in class that day, and I can't remember why. Anyway, she had us come up and stand around her desk. We were the unfortunates, meaning the overweight, the painfully shy with thick glasses, the asthmatic, and the birth marked. There were about six of us. She made us stand around her desk to watch her knit. We stood there silent and very still, for almost an hour. About halfway through, some of us were whispering to one another, and I'll never forget this as long as I live. Mrs. Otto backfisted a little girl (punched her) right in the side of the head and nearly knocked her out. As she picked herself off of the floor, she was

51

too scared to cry. Mrs. Otto went on knitting as though nothing at all had happened.

In Mrs. Otto's class, when the bell rang to signal the end of class, we would all still sit at attention waiting for her to dismiss us. One day she started yelling, "Why are you all just sitting there looking at me? Get out, class is over, and don't *make* me *tell* you to leave anymore. Do you understand?"

"Yes, ma'am, we do."

So the next day, when the bell rang, we got up and started to leave. I unfortunately sat in the first row because my last name was Clay, and she sat us in alphabetical order. About midway through the second row, she walked up and *slammed* the door shut, and we could hear her screaming. I went home and told my mom, and she said not to worry because the note was in my record. So the next day, when we entered the classroom, she was pacing back and forth with black eyes like a demon. She said to us, "All of you that did not await my dismissal yesterday are to come up front and stand in line to be paddled."

It took every ounce of courage that I had, but I stood up and said, "Mrs. Otto, you can't paddle me. I have a birthmark, and it's in my school record that I am not to be spanked."

She pointed a wicked finger at me and said, "Liar, you will get twice as many cracks from this board as the others do." And off she went, storming to the office. Well, Mrs. Otto saw that note in my school file, and my mom had also put in a call to the principal that something like this may happen, so I am sure that he informed her of it. So a miracle happened, she came crawling back into the room like a spider and started teaching class like nothing happened. I was the class hero, at least to the first row and a half. I got lots of thank yous and a few hugs.

Mrs. Otto kept houseplants along the windowsill, and the students had to water them. One day, someone watered the plant with weed killer, and they all died. No, it was not me, but I sure was happy about it.

When I was in the eighth grade, I had a bad day at school and then came home and had a major meltdown. I had major anxiety over the thought of going back the next day. One of the notorious mean boys at school (every class has one) said something mean to me about the spots on my legs. I came home, started crying (heaving), and said to my mom something like this (while crying and pitifully muttering). "Why did you have me? Why did I have to be born like this? I hate being like this. It would be better for me just to be dead. Why didn't you just let me die when I was born," and on and on.

Without blinking an eye, she said, "Well I had you. I love you, and you are here, so we will both learn to accept it and go on. What would you like for dinner? How about steak?"

After that, I always tried to remember that when people make fun of me and say mean things, it does not determine who I am. I try to not think negatively. It is a very hard thing to do when your self-esteem is taken away because the world we live in demands perfection. Don't let the roots of negativity keep you from being happy. I always practice the spirit of empathy, and I taught my son to do the same. Put yourself in someone else's shoes even for a moment and then practice the golden rule to "Do unto others as you would have others do unto you" (Matthew 7:12).

I remember watching *American Bandstand* on television every Saturday. A commercial for Nair hair removal cream would be shown just about every commercial break. It featured young girls in very short shorts. I hated that commercial. The song went "who wears short shorts, we wear short shorts, if you dare wear short shorts Nair for short shorts." I wore Bermuda shorts (they came to just above the knee) in the 1960s and early 1970s. Then they stopped making them, and the hot pants craze began. I don't know if anyone remembers sizzle suits, but they were dresses so short that your underwear was visible and your underwear matched your dress. Girls actually were allowed to wear these to school. Both styles were off limits to me, birthmark or not, although I secretly longed to wear them.

I don't really know for sure how many people at my high school knew about my birthmark. There was an incident in, I believe it was eighth grade, my home economics class. These classes were very laid back, and we sat at round tables and moved around a lot while learning to cook, etc. One day, a girl came up to me and pulled up my dress. I don't remember who it was (I actually do remember who it was but it doesn't matter), but there were a lot of gasps and girls saying ewe what is that. Needless to say, I was devastated. I wanted to say, "Oh, I was burned when I was little," because somehow in my mind that would have been a more acceptable answer. But I did not lie, I stood up straight, and I whimpered. "Oh, I just have a birthmark." Then there was pointing and giggling, and I secretly loathed those girls for a very long time. I often wonder how they knew, what made them want to pull up my dress to see the freak with the strange skin. I think it may be because I was permanently excused from gym class. I guess it doesn't matter. If I had to do it all over again, I would have handled things more differently with the knowledge that I have now. I would have explained my nevus more openly, and I would not have been upset with them. I would have given them a lesson about accepting people that were a little different from them. I would have held my head high and not have been so nervous about it all the time. What I mean is I would not have hidden the fact that I was born with a birthmark or, as Mom always said, beauty mark.

I was always very self-conscious about my nevus, and sometimes I still am. When people would ask my mom, "What is wrong with her skin?" She would just say, "She was born with a birthmark, or as I call it, a beauty mark," and then she would smile at them and change the subject. It worked, and most of the time, they smiled back. This made me more confident because I learned from watching her respond to my birthmark in a positive fashion.

In the ninth grade, all students had to take gym class; it was required to graduate. The school had a new female gym teacher. Let's call her Ms. Gym Teacher. We were required to wear a gym uniform which is OK, but it was after class that became unbearable, and horrific, and I am not talking about just me, everyone felt this way. You had to shower. However, it just wasn't showering; it was the process of showering. Ms. Gym Teacher would stand at the entrance of the shower which was one large room with no privacy partitions. She would then make you drop your towel and walk into the shower. It was humiliating. I never had to do this because my mom, upon hearing about it, got an excuse from my doctor to not participate in gym class because of my nevus. I begged for a study hall instead of going to gym class, but Ms. Gym Teacher wouldn't let me. I had to sit in the gym on the bleachers while they had class. Then I had to sit in that awful shower room until everyone was showered, dressed, and dismissed. It was beyond words awful, so I went to the principal and pleaded my case. He agreed to let me have a study hall. I don't think that this kind of behavior by a so-called educator would be tolerated in today's society. We were all just little girls going through puberty which is awful enough.

My first boyfriend, well, was a boy that was a friend of mine, I guess. I sort of liked him, but he really liked me. I was about twelve or thirteen, so what did I know? He had a curly mop of hair and wore glasses, and one day, he rode his bike all the way from Smithfield to my house in the cold. It was a long way. I remember that he had a runny nose, and my mom gave him a hot chocolate and a box of tissues. He was my first kiss. So when I was thirteen, almost fourteen, a boy from Shoaf asked me out on a date. We met at a wedding. He was my first real date because he had a real job, driver's license, a nice car, and muscles. I have no idea why my mom let me go to the movies with him because he was seventeen. He was a perfect gentleman, and we went to the movies a few times. Then he went back to his original girlfriend. No big deal, although it did sting a little because I really liked going to the movies. The original girlfriend was a classmate of mine. After she found out about me going to the movies with him, she was not happy. We were in the auditorium at school, and she was sitting behind me and decided to stick a huge wad of bubblegum in my hair. I went to my home economics teacher, and she helped me to get it out but still ended up having to cut a piece of my hair off. Gosh, that girl was irritating. They later married and divorced. Then at some point, I was asked out by a member of our basketball team. He was a very popular guy, so of course I said yes. It didn't last long, and I didn't really care. He was not all that great anyway, but most of the girls at my high school thought that he was Brad Pitt, and believe me, he was not.

Anyway, my high school years were not altogether horrible. In fact, I ran with a group of friends that were possibly the best group of friends anyone could dream of. Some went to my school, and some did not. The did-not people were cousins of my friend, Chrissy, and friends of her cousins. There were fifteen of us; however, nine of us were really close friends. We had an absolute blast, snow picnics in the mountains in the dead of winter, and Saturday night Polka dances at the Collier Fire Hall. We all went to see the movie *Young Frankenstein* at the State Theater in downtown Uniontown. We thought it was going to be scary, but it was hilarious, and we had so much fun. Gosh, I miss those days. I could write an entire book about our miscellaneous escapades because they were phenomenal. After graduating high school, we all went our separate ways, but with the Internet, especially Facebook, I am back in touch with some of them, Chrissy, Cindy, Judy, Kathy, Robbie, Gary, and Randy. Sadly, our friend, Fred, passed away a few years ago. All of my friends loved my mom, and she loved them. She always welcomed everyone to the house and was known to whip up hamburgers for everyone in a flash. She made great hamburgers. Everyone was welcome at our house, and everyone loved her.

My mom always had trouble with heartburn and tummy troubles. One day, she told me that she thought something was very wrong because she was suffering severe pain. She went to the doctor, a specialist who looked at her, and sent her to another specialist, a surgeon this time. They did a number of tests and said that she was going to need surgery as soon as possible. I was very concerned and very afraid for her. She, however, had the utmost courage. I'm sure that she was afraid also but would never share that with us. She was more worried about my dad, brother, sister, and me than she was for herself. That is just the way she was, very brave.

Growing Up Is Never Easy, Especially When It Comes to Boys, Getting Your Fist Job, and Sporting a Giant Congenital Nevus!

I'm not in love, so don't forget it
It's just a silly phase I'm going through
And just because I call you up
Don't get me wrong, don't think you've got it made.
—10 Cc, 1975

Somewhere during the year of 1974, I met, let's call him, Prince Charming. I did not particularly find him very attractive or dateable at first and had absolutely no interest in him at all. He was a friend of one of my school friends. During the summer, my group of friends wanted to take an excursion to Cheat Lake in West Virginia to go swimming. Swimming as a teenager was definitely not my thing, so I decided not to go. Prince Charming asked me if I would rather go for a ride on his motorcycle instead of going with the group, and of course I said yes. To this day, I wonder if my mother put him up to it. I didn't know it then, but this was a guy that knew all the right things to say, we got along fantastically, and soon I could think of nothing else but him. To me, the sun came up in the morning and set again at night simply because he walked the face of the earth. We saw each other every week for about a year, and I fell head over heels in love with him.

He sometimes did not treat me very nicely. I was stood up for dates more than once. He would ask me to a movie, and I would spend all day excitedly getting ready, primp, primp, primp, and then wait, wait, wait, and then he would just not show up, and I would cry myself to sleep. I can't believe I actually put up with it, but I did. One year for his birthday, I wanted to do something really special, so my mom helped me make a great dinner and a birthday cake. He was supposed to come over to my house at 6:00 p.m. I invited my friend, Chrissy, over, and she was at the time dating one of his best friends, so I invited him also. Six o'clock came and went and then seven with no phone call. He never showed up. He had no idea about the dinner as I wanted to surprise him. My parents left so that we could all have a nice evening. I cried all over Chrissy, and then I cried myself to sleep. Then the next day, he showed up at my house with profuse apologies, and everything was great again.

I had my first thoroughly serious relationship with Prince Charming. We were inseparable at that time in life, planning our life together. It would have taken a nuclear incident to blast this romance apart; that nuclear incident would happen about a year later in the form of an angelic blue-eyed blond called Cinderella. Miss Cinderella had it all, wholesomeness, beauty, porcelain skin, and great figure, she was smart, she was a ballerina, she was popular, and she walked on water.

When a girl turns sixteen, it is a very special birthday. My sixteenth birthday was a train wreck. I invited all of my friends. My mom ordered the most spectacular cake and made all the food. I was so excited, but, at the same time, I was worried. Prince Charming (let's call him PC) was acting weird, not returning calls and just not himself. He did show up, however, about an hour late. He came through the door, tossed a present at me, took a picture with me (Mom with good intentions insisted on taking that picture), and then promptly left. My mom was brokenhearted at his unexpected rudeness. She so wanted me to have a wonderful birthday. But I spent the rest of the night crying and eating copious amounts of cake and ice cream. It was the worst birthday ever. What I didn't know yet was that he had started dating Cinderella.

That breakup was brutally hard to bear. He was my world, he accepted my birthmark, and now he was gone. I thought that I would never see him again. I thought that no one in the entire world would ever fall in love with me again. I could not sleep. I could not eat. I found it hard to smile or be happy about anything. It felt like tiny little razor blades were swimming around inside my chest twenty-four seven, chopping it to pieces. It was pure misery. I did not want to go to school. I did not want to do anything. I just literally wanted to die. Then I decided to have a new beginning and break free of the misery so I cut my hair, put on makeup and moved on. I went out with almost every boy that asked, and I found something wrong with every single one of them; most never got past the first date. One guy talked with his mouth full, one guy never talked at all, one guy took me to meet his mom on our first date (creepy), one guy tried to molest me and I had to claw my way out of the car, one guy arrived thirty minutes late, I had it with guys picking me up late, so I told him to go home, and then there was the guy who showed up at my house wearing nothing but a pair of tiny shorts, eww.

I never thought I'd find anyone to fall in love with again. I could not even find someone that I liked.

Take it from me; just because you're facing a difficulty is no reason to give up on yourself. Find that opportunity that's hidden within whatever difficulty you're facing and see how you can make the most out of it (lemons to lemonade). What a difference that will make when instead of setting you back, difficulties only serve to move you forward.

I started working at age sixteen. I joined the work study program at school. We were graded on it just like a class. My very first job was at a drug store in Uniontown. I had no car, so my brother or my dad would drive me. The pharmacist that owned the business was nice, but he had a mean evil witch of a scary old woman managing it. She screamed at me from the minute I hit the door until I left. "Lorraine, why are your hands in your smock pockets? We can't have idle hands at this pharmacy." Two seconds later. "What are you doing over there? I can still see you, you know? Are you stealing? If you are stealing, I will catch you!"

My reply, "I am stocking the shelves that you wanted me to stock, ma'am." My reply in my mind, "I am stocking the shelves that you asked me to stock, Mrs. Mean, Evil, Scary Old Witch Lady." I was also very nervous and frustrated with learning the cash register and counting back money correctly. That woman would say loudly in front of the customers, "Lorraine, if you steal money from that register, I will know it. We count that register every night, so don't screw up or we will know it was you." Then on the fourth day of my very first job, I could not take it anymore. Scary Old Woman was not at work; now was my chance.

I told the pharmacist about how mean she had been treating me, and he said, "Young lady, I have had Mrs. so and so working for me for the past ten years. She runs a tight ship. Her bark is worse than her bite. Now run along and get back to the register."

I was finally relaxed at work, and then *it* happened. Some guy, about twenty years old, comes up to the counter and says, "I would like to have a pack of Natural Lamb."

I started looking through the *cigarettes*. I said to him, "I can't seem to find that brand of cigarettes."

He looks at me with a half-smile, and says, "They're not cigarettes, they are condoms."

So there I was, and I could feel my face getting redder and redder, and I went on a condom hunt. I am wishing with all of my might that Mrs. Old Evil Mean Scary Witch Lady was there. Help me, mean old lady, but she wasn't there. So I fumbled around under the counter, and there they are, condoms, Natural Lamb, with no price tag. I started to pray in my head, *Help me, Jesus, find the price tag on this pack of Natural Lamb condoms.* So I did the only thing I could and asked Mr. Condom guy. "How much do you usually pay for these?"

He gave me that same goofy look, and I rang up whatever price he quoted, and he walked out of the store with not one box but an entire carton of boxes. Mr. Condom guy must have enjoyed at least an entire year of well-protected sex before he needed to visit the drug store again.

I quit that very day. I called my brother, Joe, and I was crying so hard I could hardly get it out. "I quit my job. Please come and get me."

He did, and thank goodness I did not get in trouble at school for quitting. My next job was at Montgomery Ward, and everyone there was great.

One night, my group of friends called and invited me to go to a dance at the fire hall in West Lisenring (another coal mining patch), so I went. We were all having fun, and suddenly, there he was, walking through the door, PC, by himself. I felt like a shattered mirror, so I went outside to get some air. Well, he found me, and he was very insistent on taking me home. I told him no.

He said, "Then who do you think is going to take you home?"

Suddenly, the cute guy from the band came up and said, "I am taking her home." He was twice the size of PC. Cute guy took me home! I later found him to be undateable because he was a CB guy and always said ten four instead of goodbye on the phone. Please don't think that I am a snob, because I am not. It's just that I could not find "chemistry" with anyone else.

Chrissy called me one day and said that she had something to tell me and I needed to sit down. She told me that Prince Charming and Cinderella broke up and that he went off and joined the military. I didn't quite know how to feel about that. So I had her find out his mailing address and went on to befriend him through the mail with copious amounts of letters about small talk. I wrote to him just about every day and prayed that he would write back. My mother let me use all of the stamps that I wanted. She said rosary novenas for us to get back together at the kitchen table every night, all five decades. It worked. He wrote back, I got his much coveted high school class ring back, and as the song went, I was the happiest girl in the whole USA. So we ended up getting back together, and I was on cloud nine.

The buildup to Christmas 1978 was phenomenal. Everyone was constantly smiling and telling me that I was getting a very special Christmas present. I asked my mom for an opinion, and she agreed that I was probably about to get a marriage proposal. Even my brother said, "I think that you are getting an engagement ring for Christmas." This is what I had been dreaming of my whole life. I was so excited; I can't even begin to explain how happy I felt. PC and I would often talk about what our wedding would be like and where we would go on our honeymoon and how many children we would have and what their names would be. Now, it was all about to happen for real. I started reading *Modern Bride* magazine and thinking about what type of wedding gown I would like to wear.

My mom said, "You are going to have a big wedding just like Mary Katherine had." Even though she was very sick, she was so happy. Her surgery was scheduled for January 1, 1979.

I was very close to his family. They became a really large part of my life. They were my second family. So Christmas came that year, and I was so excited I could hardly breathe. Christmas Eve started out with dinner at my house which consisted of pea soup, fruit, fish, and tradition. Catholics don't eat meat on Christmas Eve, at least not in any Czechoslovakian or Polish household. The tradition was pea soup and oplatki which was purchased from our church every year. Google oplatki, and you will be amazed at what you'll find. You can actually still buy it online which fascinates me. Honey had to be on the table, a dollar under the tablecloth. They all had meaning, and I wish that I had paid more attention to the stories. One of them I remember; you were not supposed to leave the table for any reason until the meal was finished by everyone. It was said that the person who left the table would not be at the table next Christmas. My mother left the table; I can't remember why.

Then we drove to his sister's house and had a really nice evening. Later, we were alone in the kitchen, and he hands me this little box. When I opened it, I saw either the world's smallest engagement ring or the largest preengagement ring I have ever seen. There was no down on one knee no proposal. I didn't know what to say or how to act. You see, my heart was a little broken. I wondered if he could ever been in a truly committed relationship with me. Of course I pretended that I was really happy. I started to realize later that night that he was always going to be ready to break up with me if someone better came along. After all, he did it more than once already. All week long, everyone was saying, "Let me see your ring," and then looking at me with a puzzled look. "Gee, it's pretty, but is that an engagement ring?" I really didn't know how to answer. I do have to mention though of all the negative things that PC put me though there is a list of wonderful things that he did. It's just that God had a better plan for me, and his name was Larry William Porter.

Larry

We walked on the beach beside that old hotel
They're tearing it down now
But it's just as well
I haven't shown you everything a man can do
So stay with me baby I've got plans for you.
—Billy Joel, 1986

You just never know on any given day when you wake up in the morning if something profound will occur that will change the direction of your life forever. Disco was still all the rage in February of 1979 when I met Larry William Porter. When people ask me, "How did you meet your husband?"

I love to answer, "In a sleazy bar," just to see the looks on their faces. Actually, it was at a disco dance at our local Holiday Inn. I gained admittance with one of my best friends, Delaine Johnson (she does not know about my birthmark), and more importantly, my best fake ID. You had to be twenty-one to get in, and I was eighteen. My ID said that I was twenty-three. I thought I had a snowball's chance in Hades of getting in because I actually looked like I was about fourteen, but to my shock and surprise, they let me in. There was a spinning disco ball in the middle of the crowded dance floor and really loud disco music playing. Larry came walking in with his black wavy hair and the most beautiful brown eyes I have ever seen. He was wearing a black pin stripe suit, and the whole world stopped for a minute the first time I saw him. To my surprise, he came and sat down beside me. We were married six months later, and we have been together ever since.

Now, even after thirty-nine plus years of marriage, when he and I are apart, even if it's for a few hours, we can't wait to see each other again. He is completely beautiful inside and out, and he is my inspiration, my business partner, my strength when I get scared, my encouragement, and my best friend. He is my everything and the love of my life. I can't imagine my life without him, and he is the most spectacular husband anyone could ever hope for.

One evening, we were getting dressed up all pretty to attend a function. I said to him, "Larry, can you see my birthmark through this dress?"

He answered, "What birthmark?"

I remember coming home the night I met Larry. My mother was sitting at the kitchen table saying her rosary as she usually did every night. I said to her, "Mom, I met a really nice boy tonight."

She could have asked me any question in the world such as what does he look like? Is he nice? How old is he? etc. Her eyes lit up, and what do you think her first question was? "Is he Roman Catholic?"

When I answered yes, he was instantly on good terms with my mom. My mother's entire family were Catholics who married Catholics. Most of my dad's family were Catholics who married Catholics. They all had little Catholic babies that grew up and married Catholics and made even more Catholic babies and so on. Mary, Joe, and I were raised Catholic! You get the picture.

When I met Larry, I was still in a committed relationship with PC whom I was planning to marry. He was not Catholic, but my parents loved him anyway; in fact, my whole family loved him. Things became extremely complicated for me. My mom had been diagnosed with colon cancer and was very sick when I met Larry. She had her good days and also bad days. The day I met Larry; she was having a good day.

My friend, Delaine, who was the assistant manager of the dress shop I worked at said, "Hey, after work, let's go to the Holiday Inn and relax."

I told her that I could not because I needed to be with my mom, and I wanted to just go home.

Delaine said, "Hey, why don't you call your mom and see how she is feeling? You have not been out in forever, and you need a little break."

She had a point. So I called, and of course she said, "Yes, go out. I'm fine, and dad is here with me. Go and have a good time."

Away I went to the Holiday Inn which was very near to the mall that Delaine and I worked at.

Larry and I ended up talking all night, and we have so many things in common. We liked the same kind of food, loved the same movies, listened to the same music, and had suffered bad relationships, my mom was battling cancer and his dad was battling heart disease, we were both raised Catholic, we loved the mountains, I owned the record album *The Best of Bread Part 1* and he owned *The Best of Bread Part 2*, and just on and on, it was amazing. I remember him walking me to the car, and he reached out and took my hand and kissed it. I know that sounds really corny, but I thought that it was charming. He asked for my phone number, and I hesitated for an instant, but I just had to learn more about this Larry Porter person that I just met. He called me the next day, and again, we talked for hours. He was graduating from California State College (now known as California University of Pennsylvania) that summer (1979). I don't know when he found time to study because we were always together.

Our second meeting was at Delaine's house. She invited both of us, so who could say no? I could not find her house, and I had to call her from a pay phone; Larry was already there, so he ended up walking one street over to where I was parked. Just as we arrived at Delaine's house, she disappeared. I have to run an errand or some such excuse. I found myself totally alone with a stranger, so I was a bit nervous. I remember that she had a fish tank. I stared at that fish tank and thought, *What in the world am I doing here.* Then out of nowhere, Larry says, "I think I love you."

I replied, "Are you *crazy?*"

We were both a little crazy, so I ended up going to the movies with him the next week. I was officially "a cheater," and for this, I suffered tremendous guilt.

I would chat with PC on the phone like nothing was wrong. But everything was wrong. My secret went on for just a few weeks, and then, bam, I was caught. One of PC's friends saw Larry walking me to my car one evening after work. The phone call eventually came from PC, and it went like *blah, blah, blah, blah*. I confessed, and he was not happy. Neither was I. I was miserable.

I thought, *Where were you, Larry Porter, when I was alone, miserable, and despondent? Everything would have been so wonderful if I had met you then.*

PC came home to Pennsylvania the next weekend. In fact, on Sunday, when he left in the afternoon, Larry showed up at my house that evening. My brother said to me, "Lori, you just can't do this to these two young men. You have to make a decision." And he was 100 percent correct, so I did.

The thought that if you are truly in love with someone, you will not be drawn to anyone else is not always valid in reality. It really is possible to be in love with more than one person; for me, it was torment. I remember whining to one of my girlfriends. "What should I do? This is so horrible. I don't want to hurt either one of them."

She replied, "Oh, poor you, you have two exceedingly wonderful men that want to marry you. I can't even get a date." She had a point. Both knew about my disfiguring birthmark, and both still loved me for being me. It is extremely hard to find someone that is not superficial. I found two of them, unfortunately, at the same time.

So I said to myself, *Lori, take a step back, understand the feelings you are experiencing, and decide who to commit to.* It was not clear; so to aid me in my decision, I made a Ben Franklin list. Why call it a Benjamin Franklin list? It is said that Ben, when faced with a decision that he was on the fence about, would take a piece of paper, fold it in half lengthwise, and put a plus and a minus sign at the top. In his genius, he discovered that by listing all the positive elements on one side and the negative things on the minus side, the decision would become obvious. It worked. I chose Larry. Yes, Larry was pleasantly persistent. I am smiling right now because I am remembering how cute he was.

It went like this. "Will you marry me?"

My reply, "No."

The next day, "I want to marry you."

My reply, "Are you *crazy*? No! You don't even know me."

The next day. "Let's get married."

My reply, "*No*, stop asking."

In actuality, I thought it was sweet that he kept asking. He asked me every single day, sometimes twice a day, sometimes twice an hour, until I finally said yes! We met in February of 1979, and we were married that same year in August.

At some point along this journey, my parents saw that Larry just may be the one for me, and they must have been worried that he would reject me after finding out about my nevus. So unknown to me, they pulled him aside one day and told him all about it. I did not find out about this until three years after we were married, and I was stunned. Larry said that after the explanation my mother gave, my dad just shook his head sadly and said, "We just don't know why this happened to her." Imagine their surprise why Larry told them that he knew about it and that I had pulled my shirt up and showed him the birthmark months ago. Larry said that they were, essentially, relieved and happy.

The reason we planned a wedding so quickly was that my mom was becoming very ill and was in and out of the hospital and had many more worse days than better days. She always said to me that since she had me so late in life, she hoped to live long enough to see me get married. So we planned for an August wedding. Larry grew up with the parish of the historic church of Saint Peter in Brownsville, Pennsylvania. He attended eight years of Catholic school and was certain that he would grow up and have his wedding ceremony in that beautiful church. It was the first Catholic parish in Fayette County. The first mass in Brownsville was held beneath the site of St. Peter's Church by a French chaplain on July 1, 1754. This is the first recorded religious service of any kind in Brownsville. The Pennsylvania Courts of the Catholic Daughters of America commemorated the mass of the French troops in glass in the large facade window in the church. This church that was such a huge part of Larry's life was added to the national register of historic places in 1980.

However, my mother's health started to decline quickly, so we both decided to move the ceremony to my church which was Saint Helen's in Shoaf. I used to walk to church; that is how close it was to my house. My mother, I, my brother, and sister were all baptized there in the original church. My sister was married in the original church as were my parents. My son was baptized in the new church. The original church burned down in 1972, and a modest modern structure was built to replace it in 1973. As I wrote earlier, the Frick Coal Company opened the Shoaf mine in 1905, and before long, there were two hundred Catholics in the surrounding area. In 1910, the pastor of Saint Cyril and Methodius Catholic Church in Fairchance was asked to do something for the Catholic families of Shoaf and its surroundings. In August of 1911, the first mass was held in one of the company houses in Smiley, and the making of a parish church was started. I wonder if it was my house. The Frick Coal Company donated the land at Shoaf for the church and donated one thousand dollars which was a fortune back then. In early December of 1913, the church was dedicated for its first service. Larry and I were married in that little church, which was packed with family and friends, on August 25, 1979. Mom, however, was too ill to attend. She was hospitalized at Mon General in Morgantown, West Virginia. It was a bittersweet day for all of us.

We had the reception of around one hundred people at the Chabanik home (up the hill) where my Aunt Connie lived at the time. My mother's sisters and sisters-in-law did all the cooking. My Aunt Irene did the decorating and baked the most delectable and beautiful wedding cake. Their friends got everything set up at the house while we were in church. One person I remember helping out with everything including serving the food was my sister-in-law, Carol Boni-Clay's mother, Barbara Boni. It was so nice of Mrs. Boni and all the other people who helped, served, cooked, cleaned, decorated, sacrificed, and bent over backward to give Larry and I a wonderful wedding. The food was spectacular, and everyone came from far and near to share in our special day. After we ate, it was time to hop in the car and head to Morgantown which back then was a little over an hour away. Our photographer came with us to take pictures of Larry and I with mom and dad. She looked so much better, and she wore her corsage on her robe. She was so happy and walked us to various rooms of other patients saying, "This beautiful bride is my daughter." She really delighted in the oohs and ahs from the entire hospital including the staff. It lightened everyone's spirit to see a bride and groom walking around the entire floor. She was always so proud of me, and I think that is partially why I am a confident mature woman today. She and my husband, Larry, have always been among my loudest cheerleaders.

We spent about an hour or so at the hospital and left Mom with a tape recorder of the ceremony; back then, there were no videos, only movie cameras that required a screen. After we returned, we made our way to the Holiday Inn in Uniontown where we met. It made sense to spend our wedding night at the place we met. What didn't make sense was telling everybody! So on about 11:00 p.m. or so, my brother, Joe, Carol, and their friends, Judy and Charlie (I think that they were all a little tipsy) came singing and pounding on our door. The thing is, we were not there. We had gone out to get a late night snack and came back to the hotel to see them all standing there banging on the door. Still makes me laugh thinking about that.

OK, so here is how we spent our wedding night. Got to the hotel, showed up in our wedding attire, this is a dumb thing to do, never do this because you become a spectacle, and made our way to our room.

The *very first* thing that we did was count our money, of course, and we had a huge box of wedding cards. We sat and read every one and could not believe how generous everyone was. Then we ventured out to the only place in Uniontown that was open late at night, Kentucky Fried Chicken, and brought it back to the room. This is when we discovered that we had visitors. Glad we had a bucket of chicken, fed visitors, got rid of visitors, and talked until 2:00 a.m. It was a long day, but you have all sorts of energy when you are young, and we were extremely young. We woke early the next day and started our honeymoon trip to Ocean City, Maryland. I was so excited to show Larry the ocean because he had never seen it;

other than that, it was a somber honeymoon. We were only there about three days, and when we arrived back, my mother had become gravely ill. We were married August 25, and my mother went to the Lord October 21, 1979.

January 1, 1979

For if we live, we live to the Lord, and if we
die, we die to the Lord. So then, whether we live or
whether we die, we are the Lord's. (Romans 14:8)

This is a very difficult chapter for me to write.

January 1, 1979, we (Joe, Carol, Mary, I, and Dad) were all in Morgantown, West Virginia, at Mon Valley Hospital. This was my mom's surgery day. Even though Tarus and Tanya were still very young, my sister flew up from North Carolina to be there for Mom and for all of us. The doctor told all of us previously that there was a 90 percent chance that they would find cancer. It was a very long surgery lasting several hours. Finally, the doctor came in and told us that she came through the surgery just fine and awoke with a perfect Hail Mary prayer. He said that he removed an incredibly large tumor weighing almost ten pounds. It was malignant, and the cancer had spread to her lymph nodes and would most likely travel throughout her body. The word malignant resonated through the room; it echoed in my brain. Then came the morbid sadness, which I had never felt before. I can't remember who said it, but I think it was my brother, Joe, who asked, "How long does she have?" The surgeon answered three weeks to six months. Dad started to weep, and then we all followed suit as the doctor said that he was very sorry and then left the room. It was the single worst day of my entire life. The restrooms were very far away, and I just barely made it before becoming violently ill.

We could go back to see her in the intensive care unit one at a time. But when it was my turn (I was eighteen), they let my brother go in with me. Joe had the monitors all figured out. "See that top number, Lori? That is Mom's blood pressure, and the number below is her heartbeat. The numbers below her heartbeat tell you how asleep she is. When they get higher, she is more awake."

I remember the loud beeping of machines and a lot of very sick people. We sat with her a while. My brother did not want to leave the hospital that day. He ended up staying there with her all night long. She was in and out of sleep. The next day, we all came to visit. She had a hose in her nose to her stomach, and a huge incision across her tummy held together with staples and stitches. Every night, they came to give her an injection in her stomach very close to her incision. She never complained.

A few days later, when she recovered enough from the surgery, the doctor came in to tell her what he found. He gently explained everything to her and said, "Mrs. Clay, you will need to go home and get your house in order."

My mother was an intelligent woman, but she was also very literal. When she heard those words, she thought that he was telling her that she was well enough to go home and clean the house! So she did, a little at a time after she got some strength back. She promised my sister that if she lived through the surgery and got better, she would get on an airplane and fly to North Carolina to visit her. So mid-March 1979, Mom, Dad, and I were at the Pittsburgh airport boarding a plane. Mom was so nervous she was reading a magazine upside down. It was a very cold March, and they had to deice the plane which would make anyone nervous.

She was so happy to finally see my sister's home and get to visit with everyone. We were there for three days, and even though she was in pain, she had a wonderful time. We even went to the North Carolina Zoo which back then was in early development, and it was very small. If I remember correctly, Mom got peed on by a hippopotamus, and we all had a good laugh. When we got back home, the chemo began; she became quite ill and was in and out of the hospital a lot. I remember one time we went to Morgantown by ambulance. I rode with her, and she asked if the driver would turn the siren on so that she could hear it, so they did; it made her smile.

Then the big pain came, the kind that won't go away even with morphine. There were no colonoscopy procedures back then. There were no ports for chemo or injections. There was morphine, and, thankfully, we had a doctor that gave her all she needed. But it had to be injected, and she ended up with needle marks everywhere. It was awful. Her chemo was experimental, and it did not work at all; it just made her even worse. Then one day, she had to go into the hospital, and she never came back home because she went into a coma. The doctor called us to come in and stay with her because she was very near death. Joe, Carol, Larry, and I spent the entire day at the hospital by her side. She did not move, she was barely breathing, and we wondered if she was still in pain. The nurses brought her pain meds as usual. Later in the day, Larry and I left, and I cried all the way home. Joe and Carole stayed, and about four hours after we arrived home, we got the call that she had passed. My brother said that she took one huge breath, and then she was gone. He was holding her hand. And so her suffering was over, and I was weirdly relieved and totally devastated all the same time.

My cousin, Carole, lost her dad not too long ago to cancer. He was my mom's brother, Max, he had a big personality, and everyone loved him. She asked me, "Lori, when does it stop hurting this much?"

I answered, "It doesn't, and you just learn to deal with it better day by day."

I remember the first day of visitation at the Wagner and Cooley Funeral home in Fairchance, Pennsylvania. I was inconsolable, and if it had not been for Larry, I don't know how I would have gotten through it. I became ill as we made our way to Uniontown, and we had to stop at the mall where I worked so that I could throw up before we continued on our way to the funeral home. We got there late, and you know because of the nevus how I feel about people looking at me, and everyone was looking at me, of course. So we made our way into the room, and there was Mom. She looked like she was sleeping very peacefully. She had not slept peacefully for several years. And she was surrounded by roses, and they were beautiful, just like she had been a beautiful rose her whole life. My sister came up to comfort me, and I did OK. There were a lot of people there that evening and every evening. Larry and I sat in an adjacent room with my cousin, Carole, and her husband, Joe, and they were a great source of comfort for us.

One Saturday morning, in March of 2017, came the worst phone call ever. My beloved cousin, Carole, died from cardiac arrest. It was sudden, and it was incredibly hard to bear the loss of her. I lost my cousin, my dearest friend, and a little piece of myself. She had the most beautiful smile and giggle, and when I think of her, I can hear her laughing and telling me some type of humorous story. She always made me smile, and she lit up every room she walked into. She was loved by everyone, and I miss her so very much. She read my story (as much as I had written back then) and gave me a shining review which my heart treasures. She saw my birthmark plenty of times but never blinked an eye. I am a better person for having known her, and she helped me build confidence without ever knowing it.

I grew up alongside of my cousin, Carole. Max (my mother's brother) was married to my Aunt Lee, and they had five children, Bill, Bob, Joanie, Barb, and Carole. They lived in Smithfield on a farm that was literally at the foot of the mountain. Carole is a year or two older than me, but we were always pals. Going to visit my Uncle Max and Aunt Lee was such a treat for me while growing up. Mom would call outside. "We're going to Uncle Max's house." I would run in squealing with delight. We would stay for hours sometimes, and it was always an adventure. We would run and play in the pasture, and one time, Barb and Carole wanted to show me where a cow had given birth. They explained the process with disgusting detail and equal facial expressions of sheer dismay. When we found that nothing was there any longer, we decided to take a shortcut through the barbed wire fence.

Barb and Carole had it down to a science but me, not so much. Barbara held the top strings of wire, and Carole held the bottom and said, "OK, just step on through." Well, it goes without saying that I did it, of course, and I cut my leg on the wire. Aunt Lee put mercuro-chrome on it. For the young folks reading this, mercurochrome was a red liquid to keep out infection, and it was like liquid fire. It healed nicely, and I never told my mother.

One summer, I stayed a few days at Uncle Max's house, and my dad let me bring my bicycle. Carole and I rode our bikes all over Smithfield including rock hole where we went wading in the water with our shorts folded up as high as we could get them. I remember thinking in my ten-year-old mind that maybe these are magical waters that will take away my birthmark, at least the parts touching water. Then I thought if this magical water removes the birthmarks from my legs, I'm going to come here and soak my entire body. My immediate next thought was of snakes. Thank goodness we did not see any snakes because that location is crawling with copperheads. We played badminton a lot, had huge monopoly games, and played records, and Carole could play piano, so I would beg her to play for me, and she would. I slept in a full-size bed between Barb and Carole, and every morning, as the sun came up, the rooster would do his cock a doddle doo thing. It scared me to death the first time I heard it.

Carole married Joe a year after Larry and I married, and I was a bridesmaid in her wedding. Larry and Joe became fast friends, and Larry and I are godparents to their first child, Laura. Carole and Joe are godparents to our son, Michael. After Larry joined the Navy and we moved away, we don't see them very much, but when we did, it is always wonderful.

My mother had a lovely church service at Saint Helens in Shoaf where in the original church she was baptized, had her first holy communion and confirmation, and was married. The church was packed with friends and relatives. Then there was that terrible trek to the cemetery. I love cemeteries, but I hated Saint Joseph's on that day. My dad passed away six months after her, and I lost my dear Aunt Connie too. It was a rough year.

After my dad passed away, we moved from our little apartment in Uniontown back to the house in Shoaf. I wondered if I would really ever live anywhere else.

Baby Makes Three

Hey you, you're a child in my head
You haven't walked yet
Your first words have yet to be said
But I swear you'll be blessed

I know you're still just a dream
your eyes might be green
Or the bluest that I've ever seen
Anyway you'll be blessed

I'll pick a star from the sky
Pull your name from a hat
I promise you that, promise you that, promise you that
You'll be blessed.

—Elton John, 1995

Somewhere around August 1980, we decided to start a family. Friends of ours had the cutest baby girl, and we loved visiting them so that we could play with her. Larry and I discussed it at length and talked about how many couples try for months and sometimes years to have a child. Well, it took us about twenty-eight days! Suddenly, I was expecting. Billions of women have babies and live through it right, so how hard could childbirth actually be, right?

I *hate* going to new doctors. I never know how they are going to react to seeing my nevus. Nevus Outreach, Inc., published a brochure explaining all about large nevi and related disorders. I am so thankful to them for this brochure. I wish I would have had it all my life.

There were not many physicians to choose from in Uniontown, Pennsylvania. I can't really remember that well, but I think that there were two obstetricians. They were both female. One was very mean, and I only heard horrendous things about her and the way she treated her patients; however, she had a great deal of experience, and she was a very learned physician. The other was the one I chose; she was new in town, but I only heard great things about her. I asked her about natural childbirth classes.

You know how I feel about needles, so I asked Larry if he would mind going to natural childbirth classes with me. He loved the idea, so we went. We met at the home of a nurse that was the instructor at her home in Uniontown on Wednesday nights at 6:00 p.m. There were about six couples signed up for the program. It was a good program, but they laid it on the line about what happens *exactly* when you have a baby. We had to do exercises, and some of them involved us getting on the floor and doing silly things that were supposed to teach us something about how to breathe and control pain. A few of us got to giggling because we all looked like beached whales. Ms. Nurse Instructor did not like it and said, "You won't be giggling when you are in unbearable pain, screaming for death while pushing out these babies." That statement made us listen very intently. There was not much fun in this class, but nonetheless, we attended every one of them.

Larry and I were so excited. We would stay up late and talk about the baby and about what he or she would be named. They did not have ultrasound in 1981. We wanted an Irish name, so if it was a boy, he would be Shawn Michael, Clay Michael, or Michael Shawn. A girl would have been Katherine Rose (named for my sister, Larry's sister, Cathy, and my mom).

Our son arrived two weeks past my due date. I was certain that I was going to be huge and pregnant forever. I was so huge that I could hardly breathe. The baby would put its feet up against my rib cage and stretch about once an hour. Larry had to put on my shoes. When my father in law would see me, he would sing the baby elephant walk. You know it, "Du du dut du du du du du daaa" and on and on actually made me laugh. He used to call me Ordie because that is the name that my little nephew, David, gave me when he was two.

Everyone called Larry's dad pap. One day, Pap said, "Hey, Ordie, you look like you swallowed a watermelon." And that would make me laugh. He also would say, "Hey Ordie, you have chipmunk cheeks. Looks like you are storing nuts for winter." That would make me laugh too. My father-in-law, Ralph Porter (Pap), was such a great man. He lit up a room just from walking in. We miss him so much. Larry is the old pap pap now.

Every night, in my prayers, I asked the Lord to time my going into labor after I had a good night's sleep, and that is exactly what happened. Early Sunday morning, June 14, 1981, I woke up in labor. It was Larry's turn to do the readings in church that Sunday at St. Helens. I told him to go ahead and go because we were told in class that first-time mothers can be in labor for sometimes an entire day. He went, and I took a shower and made sure everything was just right with the house and also that I packed everything that I needed. I was so excited. By the time he got home, the pains were about five minutes apart. I called my brother to tell him I was in labor. He wanted to come to the hospital to be there for us, but it was Carol's surprise baby shower day, and I did not want him to miss it. So off to the hospital we went. We were there all alone because Larry's mom (against the protests of Larry and his dad) decided to go off to Ohio to visit relatives. And that was just as well because Larry was with me every minute anyway.

We arrived at the Uniontown hospital at about one in the afternoon, and my labor went really quick. I went from being uncomfortable to feeling real pain and then indescribable pain that was mind-bendingly horrific. I had no meds, doing it like in the olden days. I don't know how I talked my obstetrician into it, but I had no IV. No one was putting a needle in my birthmark in my back, no epidural, no way. I screamed a lot. They closed my door and told me that I was scaring the other women; I did not care about the other women. I prayed for death (just me not the baby). Larry was a fantastic coach. He was by my side every second. I got back rubs and foot rubs, and he would do the breathing thing with me and encouraged me that everything was going to be alright, and we prayed together. I was still scared, and I wanted my mother. Larry was the next best thing, but I think that all women want their mothers to be with them through labor and delivery. I was so glad that I had such a great husband; most men at that time would in no way go into the labor and delivery room.

I had a multitude of nurses, and of course they all see you naked. After a while, I didn't care at all because I was at my wits end. They all reacted to my birthmark in different ways. Some looked amazed, some were puzzled, most acted like it was not there, and I liked them the most. No one asked me any questions about it. I had nasty nurses, and I had angelic nurses. The nasty nurses would shout out like a Marine gunnery sergeant. "You better relax your face muscles, be quiet, and save your strength because the *real* pain hasn't even set in yet." I remember the angelic nurses the most; they would speak softly and say things like, "Just think in just a little while you will be holding your beautiful little baby." That helped so much because I started to focus on why I was there.

By seven in the evening, it was time to push out the baby because, guess what, the baby was coming, and I was not even pushing. Once my water broke, the baby was swimming on out, and everyone went into action. There were people running all over the place because my doctor was not there yet. They were telling me, "Don't push," and I was like, *I'm not pushing,* but the baby is *coming out.* I remember Larry having to gown up, and suddenly he is running beside my gurney, and we were all running to the delivery room. I heard my doctor's heels on the hard hospital floor, clop, clop, clop, clop, as she was running to catch up with us. The table they put me on actually had straps on it. A male orderly said to me, "If you are a good girl, we won't have to strap you down." That was a little unnerving.

The obstetrician said, "OK, let's have this baby!"

I was finally allowed to push. For me, pushing out a baby was no problem. I watch women on television having babies, and it's like they can hardly push. I was a mighty pusher, and I think it is because I had no meds. Larry was standing on my right. I was looking at him, and all of a sudden, he drops down to my face and says, "Just look at me, and everything will be OK."

I was puzzled, so I looked up at the doctor, and she was filling up this extremely long needle and did the squirt thing out of the top. I proceeded to lose my mind. *"No!"* I tried to climb off the table, and Larry and three nurses and one male orderly held me down.

My doctor said, "Just a little sting. We have to numb you for the episiotomy."

Larry and I learned in our natural childbirth classes that you didn't need an episiotomy. It did not matter because she numbed me up and started cutting before we could protest, *and that* was when Larry lost his knees. He did not pass out, thank goodness, nor did I. Two pushes later, at exactly eighteen minutes after seven, the most beautiful baby in the whole world was born. I remember the doctor holding him up in the air, umbilical cord still attached, and she said, "It's a boy," and she kind of bounced him up and down and said, "He's a *big* boy."

Larry actually started jumping up and down saying, "We have a son. I can't believe it. It's a boy!" It was the absolute best moment of my entire life. The first thing I asked was, "Does he have a birthmark?"

The doctor said, "No, not even one." Then they took little eight-pound three and one half ounces Michael away. I asked Larry to go out and call everyone, and then I received my many stitches. It took so long that I thought she was sewing a prom dress by hand. So while I had the rest, I started wondering about how much weight I gained. Happily, I weighed one hundred and ten pounds before the baby, and by the day we brought him home, I got on the scale and looked down to see exactly one hundred and ten pounds.

All three of us got to be together in the recovery room where Larry and I got to hold him and kiss him and count fingers and toes, and we were so happy. What a wonderful feeling to give birth to a child with the person you love the most in the whole world. In the past, we had talked about having two children, so I looked over at Larry and asked, "Do I have to do this again?"

He replied with an abrupt no. That is the instant that Michael became an only child. We never regretted it because Michael was very expensive. Food, clothes, shoes, medicine, braces, toys, bikes, boy scouts, books, comic books, comic book conventions, scouting equipment, camping equipment, summer camps, karate lessons, computers, piano lessons, a new car, private college, and on and on. But he was worth it. When he was little, he would always ask if he could have a baby brother, and I said no. In the next breath, he asked for a puppy. Something tells me that this was planned. He got a puppy way back then, and now he has his own little babies to play with, our granddaughters Elizabeth Adair Porter and Katherine Rose Porter.

We brought baby Michael back to the house in Shoaf where I, my sister, and my brother grew up. We lived there as a family until May of 1983 when Larry joined the US Navy. That house is gone now, destroyed by a fire. In 2011, Larry and I took Michael and his wife, Kimberly, to visit the family where we grew up in Southwestern Pennsylvania. So naturally, we drove out to Shoaf.

I could not envision where our house once stood or the swing Dad built or the grape arbor or plum tees because everything looked so different. You can't see the railroad tracks or the coke ovens because everything is covered by trees, brush, and bushes. It gave me the strangest feeling.

Weird Things that People Have Said to Me

Be kind to unkind people; they need it the most.

"If someone murders you, the police would have no problem identifying your dead body" (nurse).

"I bet that thing keeps you warm in winter" (nurse).

"I hope that you understand that your deformity *really* bothers your husband. I mean, it *has* to." (male Harvard educated dermatologist, University of Pittsburgh). This physician wanted to make me his science project. Side note: Larry was deployed at the time of this discussion. When he returned and I told him what Dr. Rude said, he wanted to drive to Pittsburgh to pummel him.

"Did someone accidently pour iodine all over you, dear?" (nurse the day after my son was born).

The day my sweet granddaughter was born, a well-meaning family member said, "Lori, I prayed all night last night. I prayed and prayed that the baby won't have the fuzzies."

When I asked what they were talking about (because I really did not know), they said, "You know that nasty stuff that you are covered with."

"Why do you always have that cold sore on your lip, dear?" From an aunt on my dad's side of the family that I saw about every three years. She asked me every single time. I have a satellite mark on my lower lip, right side. It has faded through the years.

"How did you get splashed with tar? It washes off, you know" (stranger).

To my mother. "Well, at least she has a pretty face" (neighbor).

To my mother. "At least that awful mark is not on her face" (neighbor).

The Navy

Wanna pack your bags, Something small
Take what you need and we disappear
Without a trace we'll be gone, gone
The moon and the stars can follow the car
and then when we get to the ocean
We gonna take a boat to the end of the world
All the way to the end of the world You and me
together, we could do anything, baby
You and me together
—Dave Matthews Band, 2009

Even though this Dave Matthews song was released in 2009, it reminds me of when Larry and I left Pennsylvania, forever. It is like this song was written for us.

Late in the year 1982, Larry came home from work one day and announced to me right out of the blue that he was joining the Army.

I said, "Are you *crazy?*"

He said that we were never going to have a future living in southwestern Pennsylvania. The *last* thing I wanted in the whole wide world was to become a military wife. I guess I was destined to be one. Larry said that he talked to a recruiter and wanted to be a helicopter pilot. That is until we went to his parent's house for our weekly Sunday dinner.

Larry's dad said, "Boy, if you join anything, it's going to be the Navy." So the Navy it was! Larry's dad served in the Navy during World War II.

In our current home, Larry has a room which we affectionately call the tower. Right after we moved in and while Larry was away on a business trip, I decided to work on a surprise for him. On the focus wall I, hung the picture of his dad's ship that hung in his family's home, and I made a beautiful display of photos and mementos that belonged to Ralph Porter. I also had a picture of Larry's favorite ship, the USS Shenandoah, and framed and hung it with Larry's various awards on the other side of the focus wall. In Larry's Tower/I love Me Room, there are also commendations and medals that include but are not limited to five good conduct medals, five meritorious unit commendations, two Navy achievement medals, a Southwest Asia Defense medal, and more from the First Gulf War; they are all on display. The highest honors that he earned were three Navy commendation medals from three separate commands for his exemplary service. He was also Sailor of the Year.

Early in 1983, Larry was accepted into the Navy. My father in law drove Larry, baby Michael, and me to Uniontown and left Larry with the recruiter who took him to Pittsburgh International where he left for ten weeks of boot camp in San Diego. It was a somber day for all of us. Larry had never been on a plane before. I was numb and in semi-disbelief as we drove home. He had to spend an additional twelve weeks in San Francisco in school. We had never been apart before, and it was extremely difficult for our little family, but we were strong and everybody survived. It turned out that the Navy was an extremely good decision. It was life changing, but in a magnificently wonderful way.

Michael and I flew to North Carolina in May to spend the summer and part of the fall with my sister and her family. Michael turned two years old while we were there, and Aunt Mary bought him a monkey, Curious George. She bought me a monkey on my second birthday. I have both monkeys put away in their "greatly loved" condition. I had to sew George very carefully back together several times. As a toddler, I chewed the hand off my monkey whose name was Jo Jo. Aunt Connie sewed it back on, but it still very well chewed. The last "fix" on Jo Jo was done by my sister when she put him back into a near-perfect original condition. Michael also had his first haircut that summer; all of his curls came off. It was a really hot summer.

My niece, Tanya, was fifteen, and my nephew, Tarus, was seventeen that summer. Tanya turned sixteen in September. Then there was me at twenty-three and Michael at two. My sister had her hands full that summer. I was trying to potty train Michael, so naturally, he peed on Aunt Mary's carpet more than once. Then there was the day he figured out how to open his sippy cup and threw it at Aunt Mary's wall. Oh my, Rich and Mary both had the patience of the biblical Job. I am ever thankful to them for letting us stay with them from May to November. Larry was in boot camp and then went directly to A-School.

I missed Larry terribly, and I worried that when he came back, Michael would not remember him. That summer lasted for what felt like years to me. Don't get me wrong, I love my sister's house, but it was really hard being away from Larry and thinking about him suffering in boot camp. I begged him not to join. I didn't realize it at the time, but he made a sacrifice for us so that Michael and I could live a better life. I am ever grateful and so very proud of his naval career and numerous awards. Living the Navy life of a Navy wife made me a stronger person. I was more social, and I got to live in other parts of our great country and also across the pond in Scotland. Life became a great adventure, and I learned assertiveness and many other life skills with Larry right beside me all the way *and* much prayer.

During that summer MTV was new. I remember watching the promo with artists such as Sting from the Police and David Bowie saying, "I Want My MTV." In Pennsylvania, we had a TV antenna, three channels, and a snowy picture. My sister had something called *cable television*, and it was in *color*. MTV (Music Television) actually played music back then, and to me, it was fabulous. I remember watching Michael Jackson's Thriller for the first time. It was an MTV event, and it did not disappoint. I remember trying to do Michael Jackson's dance from the Beat It video with Tanya, and we just could not do it.

I worked for a few months at the Asheboro KMart from 5:00 a.m. to 11:00 a.m. doing stocking in the candy and toys section. I loved that job. Tanya watched Mike for me. I got to take a trip to San Francisco to see Larry at school. It was over a weekend, and I asked

Mary not to give Michael sugar or coke. She let him have both, and I am told that he ran in circles around the house until about 2:00 a.m. Never give a two-year-old sugar or coke and especially at the same time. So another few weeks passed, and Larry finally got to come home to North Carolina. He brought Michael a stuffed shark puppet/stuffed animal. He was so happy to see his daddy, and when we asked him what the shark's name was going to be, he said, "Happy." So it was settled; he would always be referred to as Happy the shark. Our first duty station was Groton, Connecticut.

Connecticut

It is God who arms me and makes my way perfect.
—Psalm 18:32

D o I get discouraged because I have a birthmark? Yes. Did my self-esteem suffer while I was growing up because I looked different from the other girls? Yes. How could it not? These feelings are normal. What is important is what I did about it. I pushed that defeated mind-set away. I embraced my problem, I kept looking forward, my cup was always half full, and I surrounded myself with good people. I think that making it through difficult times make us stronger.

I never knew about the melanoma risk involved with having a nevus until I was twenty-four years old. We were living in Gales Ferry, Connecticut, at that time; it was our first duty station with the Navy. There was a large military hospital there, so when it came time for my yearly medical exam, I made an appointment and went. I have always had a difficult time seeing new doctors because I never knew how they were going to react to my nevus. But nothing could have prepared me for what I was about to endure on this routine appointment. The physician was male, and I was n-e-r-v-o-u-s as usual. It is an awful thing to go through anyway, let alone having to go through it with a rare birth defect. So it went like this. I was escorted into the room by the *"take everything off and put this on leaving it open in the front"* person. So there I was, and the doctor came in, and I told him that I had a large birthmark, and he seemed very bored with it until he actually started the exam.

He stands up, looks at me, and says, "Do you know what you have here?"

I'm thinking, *Duh, yes, I was just telling you about it a few minutes ago.*

Then he says, "What you have here is cancer. I mean, that it is a precancerous condition. These things turn to deadly melanoma, and you probably won't live to see your fortieth birthday. You have a 10 percent chance of getting cancer. Let me get a dermatologist in here."

So as I lay there in shock, terrified because a doctor just told me I had cancer, he comes sailing into the room with not one but three other male doctors who stood and stared at me for what seemed like a millennium. They were talking and mumbling among themselves, and I was totally violated and beyond frightened. I thought, *Who is going to help Larry raise little Michael when I die? I hope I live long enough for him to be at least a teenager.* It was one of the most terrifying humiliating days of my life.

I went home and told Larry the news, and he was as shocked as I was. I cried a lot. I could not understand why my mom didn't tell me. As I think back now, I know that she was trying to protect me, and even though my brother and sister never told me, I *know* that our mother swore them to secrecy because she did not want me to worry. Mom always overprotected me. I could not learn to cook because I would burn myself, she didn't want me to help her clean the house, she would say go and play with my Barbie dolls or (when I was older) do something fun. She said, "You will have plenty of time to wash dishes when you have a husband and a home of your own." Well, now, they have machines for that and I don't wash dishes anyway! I would have liked to help her; anyway, I love to clean. Even as I am sitting here in my office, typing on this computer, I am looking around thinking, *Hmm, it would be fun to dust in here tonight.*

What I learned from this dreadful day in Connecticut is that life is very precious. As Elton John sings, "All life is precious, and every day's a prize." Ever since that day, I have strived to live every single day to the fullest. I noticed how green the grass was, how blue the sky was, and how quickly the minutes, hours, days, months, and years go by. I picked my son at daycare who was then three years old, and I hugged him and told him what a good little boy he was and that I loved him. I appreciated him more, I appreciated my husband more, and I appreciated my sister more and my entire family. I appreciated life and being well, and I embraced it. Even more than that, I strived to be the reason someone smiled each and every day. Most importantly, I gave my fear over to God, and I was instantly comforted and had no more fear.

We were stationed in Connecticut for two years. Michael was finally potty trained, so we could buy steak instead of Pampers. There was not much to do there. Our apartment complex had a huge pool, so Larry would take Michael swimming. I, of course, did not swim, but I enjoyed watching Larry with Michael.

The Naval Submarine Base at Groton, Connecticut, was established on December 7, 1941. Larry worked in submarine repair and was not a "bubble head" (submariner) but a "surface puke" (surface ship sailor). These are the terms Navy guys used for each other. Larry worked on critical piping systems, main seawater systems, and auxiliary seawater systems. He also worked in nuclear repair.

Back then, Groton was (with a small child) a thirteen-hour car trip. Nonetheless, we visited Pennsylvania once or twice a year. At the end of our two-year stay in Groton, Larry went, where else, to a school in California. Michael and I stayed with his parents. I remember answering the phone the day Larry called and said that his orders were taking us to Dunoon, Scotland. I went into an instant horrified panic attack. I did not want to go; however, our three years there was counted as sea duty although the ship did not go out very often. So that was a great blessing.

Scotland

God will be with you wherever you go.
—Joshua 1:19

Between the duty stations of Groton, Connecticut, and Dunoon, Scotland, while Larry was at a school, I stayed with Larry's parents while I sold our house in Shoaf. I guess that I was destined to become a Realtor. In 1986, the Navy took us to Dunoon, Scotland, for three years. The US Nuclear Submarine Base, Site One, Holy Loch, Scotland, was located on the southern shore of the Holy Loch for thirty-one years. The Holy Loch got its name because in the Middle Ages, a ship carrying a cargo of sand from the Holy Land sank in the cold murky waters of the loch.

The Holy Loch is surrounded on three sides by hills which protect it from the harsh Scottish weather and winds that prevail in this part of Scotland. The ship (which in 1986 when we were there was the USS Hunley) and the submarines were moored in the center of the loch for security purposes and made it difficult for terrorist or anyone else to attack. For the sailors, it was pure misery to walk to the end of the very long pier and get on a little boat that carried them to the ship and dry dock; my husband was one of them.

In autumn, 1959, the United States government had to provide forward servicing facilities for the first fleet ballistic missile submarines (SSBN) nuclear squadron to be based in the United Kingdom, and studies were carried out to determine the most suitable location for such a refit facility, leading to the final selection of the Holy Loch in July 1960. Site One became fully operational in November 1961.

The area offered deep, sheltered access and had already seen service during World War II, as a Royal Navy submarine base.

So let me start at the beginning of our journey. Michael was four years old. I was terrified. I did not want to live in a foreign country. I would have rather stuck a fork in my eye than leave the United States. There was a lot of preparation including a physical and psychological exam for both Michael and I. I was very nervous about showing military physicians my birthmark. We had to drive to Pittsburgh for the exams. Larry's dad went with us, and when we arrived, he found a lobby full of WWII vets, and he was in heaven, so he remained in the lobby. To my dismay, Michael and I passed all the exams. To my utmost delight, they did not make me take off my clothes! I later found out that if we would not have passed, they would have sent Larry anyway "unaccompanied," and that would have been dreadful.

The Chernobyl disaster occurred on April 26, 1986 in Ukraine which was a part of the Soviet Union back then. We left for Scotland mid-May and were exposed to it. The fire released large quantities of radioactive particles into the atmosphere and created a dispersal of a radioactive cloud which drifted not only over Russia, Belarus, and Ukraine but also over Europe including Turkey, Greece, Moldova, Romania, Bulgaria, Lithuania, Latvia, Finland, Denmark, Norway, Sweden, Austria, Hungary, Czechoslovakia, Yugoslavia, Poland, Estonia, Switzerland, Germany, Italy, Ireland, Slovenia, France, Canada, and *the United Kingdom*. I don't want to even think about how much exposure we received while in the air flying to Ireland and then Glasgow, Scotland. Not good for anyone but especially not good for a nevus wearer or a small child. Mandatory radioactivity testing of sheep in parts of the United Kingdom that graze on lands with contaminated peat was lifted in 2012. They were testing sheep for a very long time.

So off to Scotland we went in May of 1986. I had never had a fear of flying because I flew to North Carolina when I was a child. I did, however, have a fear of getting on that plane with our four-year-old son. I remember being very ill that day because I was so frightened especially about the nuclear disaster in Kiev (Ukraine). Larry's dad drove us to Pittsburgh International, and I was sick the whole way there. We flew to New York and had a two-hour wait before boarding our connecting flight to Ireland where we landed for refueling. Back then, the flight took about seven hours and then another hour to Glasgow, Scotland. Halfway across the Atlantic, the plane started to pitch and sway and shake, and I remembered looking over at little sleeping Michael holding his curious George monkey that Aunt Mary gave him for his second birthday and thinking at least he will be asleep and not frightened when we all die. I saw the flight attendants seat belting themselves which really made me nervous. The plane took a slight dive straightened out and then pitched around for ten minutes which to me was like ten hours. But everything was OK, and we landed safe and sound. We were tired and did not know what to expect when we arrived. It was like landing in another world. I remember using the restroom, and I did not know how to flush the toilet. I figured it out though (and I was only operating on half a brain right then) there was a chain hanging in the air and you had to pull down on it.

From the airport, we had to board a bus for an hour commute and then get a taxi so that we could board a ferry to Dunoon and then we were finally there. You know how in America you step out and hail a cab? In Scotland, everyone lines up in what they refer to as a queue. Larry and I did not even notice said queue and hailed a cab the American way. As we got in, there was shouting (about the queue) by some very disgruntled people, and we had no idea why. All in all, the entire trip from Pittsburgh to Dunoon took about fifteen hours. We ended up in a very nice bed and breakfast for about two months, and that is where we met our wonderful friends, Neal, Violet, and wee Susan who we remain in touch with today.

We were advised as new arrivals to purchase wellington boots. It rains a lot in Scotland, and by a lot, I mean almost all the time. We were also advised to sight see in the rain. Also sound advice because if we had not toured in the rain, we would have never gone anywhere. This was told to us again and again, so one of our fist ventures out was to the Ardnadam complex which was across from the ship, the USS Hunley, which sat in the dry dock. It was American, and we could pay for our wellington boots (wellies) with US dollars.

There was a guy in line that looked at me and asked, "So where are you from, in the states?"

I answered, "Uniontown, PA, which is about halfway between Pittsburgh and Morgantown, West Virginia."

He said, "I thought you had some kind of uneducated hillbilly accent."

I did not know quite how to answer. Turned out he was kidding because he too was from the same area.

After procuring the much coveted wellie boots, we made our way to Benmore Botanic Gardens. There aren't many trees in that part of Scotland, the Cowal Peninsula (compared to the United States), but there are oodles of trees at Benmore. Lots of trails to walk, and it was so peaceful and spectacular all at the same time. We ventured to the botanical gardens many times during our three years in Scotland. All of Scotland is enchantingly beautiful, and the landscape is green with rolling hills, dramatic cragged mountains, coasts, and islands; the highlands are home to several stunning oak woodlands that are often referred to as Celtic rainforests and are home to abundant flora and are carpeted in soft layers of mosses, liverworts, and lichens. Like a fairytale.

The list for Navy housing was very long, and the wait was about six months. We could stay in the bed and breakfast for up to two months. So in the meantime, you had to live on the Scottish economy. We had to find a rental and pay for it with British currency. It was expensive even for really small houses with holes in the walls they called fireplaces that you had to burn coal in, and they were in every room. If you found a place with central heating, you were really fortunate. We looked high and low and finally found a very nice house with three bedrooms and one bath. The heating consisted of weird radiators. They were filled with some sort of bricks that warmed up when you turned on the switch that was on the side. They never really got that warm. There were two in the house which was built of stone, and you had to sit on top of them to get warm, and I did. Then we found out about calor gas heaters. They are much like our kerosene heaters we have in the United States. We had three calor gas heaters.

On the Fourth of July 1986, we heard that the Americans were hosting fireworks over the Firth of Clyde. Larry was on the ship standing duty. We lived only one block back from the water in our Scottish house, so when 10:00 p.m. approached, little Michael and I walked over to the benches that lined the waterway. To my surprise, no one was sitting on the benches. I noticed that there were cars parked everywhere with people in them, and I started to wonder why. Soon, I noticed little tiny flying bugs; they were like pepper with teeny wings, and all at once, we were swarmed. So we *ran* while I swatted bugs away from my five-year-old son. I imagined all of those cheeky people laughing as we escaped. I later found out that the little bugs are called midges, and they attack in clouds.

Scotland is so far north that there is daylight for eighteen hours during the summer. I remember Larry cutting the grass at 11:30 p.m. in June while battling the midges. He would wear a jacket with a hood and tie it tightly around his face and apply midge cream to the few exposed parts. In fact, in June, it really never gets dark; hence grass cutting at almost midnight. You could read your favorite book outside at 3:00 a.m. There is only about five or six hours of daylight in winter which made me very cranky. On most days, you barely had real daylight. The climate was so cold and damp living there that we had to wear winter clothes almost year round.

In Great Britain (at least back then), everyone had tiny little refrigerators. Because of this, women would push their children in strollers (prams) to the market every day. It would start about 8:00 a.m. I would hear them in their heels walking to the market. That's right, heels; no sneakers were worn by Scottish women back then. Our bedroom was next to the sidewalk near downtown Dunoon. We, Americans, could borrow a regular-sized American refrigerator run through a converter box, so that is what we did.

We lived on the Scottish economy for around six months, and then we moved into Navy housing at Innellan Park. We were ecstatic because it was housing reserved for military members with a rank of E-7 and up; Larry was an E-5 back then. Innellan had true central heating (oil). We were very fortunate to get the nicest housing that they had to offer. They were one-story homes with two bedrooms, one bath, a living room, a dining area, and a kitchen; Neal, Violet, and wee Susan lived there also. Michael and Susan became pals, and there were a lot of children in the neighborhood which consisted of about twenty-four houses. They all attended Innellan Primary which was established in 1868 and was a stone building at the top of a hill that had no indoor bathrooms. The bathrooms were outside the building.

The town of Innellan itself was quaint, quiet, and utterly beautiful. We went exploring one day and decided to drive as far as we could because at the end of the road (one track), there was nothing because we were on a peninsula. There was a mansion back there that was rumored to be where Sting came to write and record music. It was huge and had a huge fence around it. We lived at the beginning of the neighborhood, and it was one block away from the Firth of Clyde. We often went to the rocky beach, and on a clear day, you could see Ailsa Craig which is a small island formed from the volcanic plug of an extinct volcano. The road from Dunoon to Innellan runs along the Firth of Clyde. I walked for exercise every day along the sidewalk of that road and the breath taking scenery. It's a great memory; however, I started to have a lot of itching on my birthmark. Itching turned into pain. It took the longest time to figure out that my back was receiving windburn. Even with a heavy coat on, my skin would become irritated.

Our first visitors were Larry's sister, Cathy, and her son, David, who at the time was eight years old. It was the summer of 1986. We were living in our Scottish house built of stone that was over one hundred years old, so they got the true Scottish experience.

We took Cathy and David to the town of Inveraray. Larry, Michael, and I loved going to Inveraray, and we went quite a bit while living in Scotland. The town is called the gateway to the highlands, and it was one of the towns that we visited first when we arrived in Scotland. Inveraray Castle is my all-time favorite because it looks like a fairytale, so enchantingly beautiful. It is the ancestral seat of the Dukes of Argyll, whose family has resided in Inveraray since the early fifteenth century. The castle was built between 1745 and 1790. In 2012, the Christmas episode of *Downtown Abbey* was partly filmed at Inveraray Castle. The Thirteenth Duke and his family still live in private apartments occupying two floors

We also took Cathy and David to Edinburgh. Edinburgh has many historic buildings, including Edinburgh Castle, Holyrood Palace, and St. Giles Cathedral. Edinburgh is the capital city of Scotland and has been since at least the fifteenth century. It was my favorite city to visit. The earliest known human habitation in the Edinburgh area was a Mesolithic campsite dated to 8500 BC. Castle rock is a volcanic plug in the middle of Edinburgh, and it is the rock on which Edinburgh Castle sits. The rock is estimated to have risen some 350 million years ago. Edinburgh Castle is a historic fortress which dominates the skyline of the city of Edinburgh from its position on the 260 feet above the landscape. It was breathtaking, and I could not believe how majestically huge it was. I remember touching the walls everywhere we visited and just being in awe of the history.

Cathy and David also got to see the Cowal Highland Gathering. The Cowal Highland Gathering is held every year in Dunoon, Scotland. Thousands of people travel from all over the world to attend. There are world-class competitors in Highland dancing, pipe bands, wrestling, heavy athletics, children's entertainment, and local food. I enjoyed the dancing the most. There was a huge parade down the main street of Dunoon with pipe bands, and it was fun; I love parades. Seeing the American sailors in kilts tossing the caber was interesting, and no, Larry did not participate nor did he ever wear a kilt. Michael, however, wore a kilt to church every Easter Sunday that we lived in Scotland.

In February of 1988, I found a small hard knot on my back on my birthmark. It was on the right side of my lower back. While having a routine physical at the Site One, Holy Loch, naval clinic, I showed it to the physician. He said that I should go to Glasgow to see one of the top dermatologists in the world who happened to specialize in giant nevus research. That is when I met Professor Rona M. Mackie, professor of dermatology, Glasgow University. The doctor at the clinic made the appointment, and a few weeks later, Larry and I were on the ferry over to Gourock and then a car trip to Glasgow which took about an hour.

Glasgow University Hospital was huge and foreboding yet quite beautiful. I am glad that we got there early, and we found our way to the correct check-in area. We waited in a little room to see Professor Mackie. I was quite surprised to see a very young man walk in who happened to be studying medicine there in the dermatology department. When we asked about Professor Mackie, he said that he always screens her patients first. Then he asked me to raise my shirt so that he could see my little spot. I'll never forget those words; the look he had on his face as he went running from the room to get Professor Mackie was priceless.

Five minutes later, a very friendly motherly type woman walked into the room. She had very kind eyes and examined me from head to toe. Rona Mackie was the first female professor of dermatology in the United Kingdom and was the first woman to be appointed to an established chair in the University of Glasgow. She is an expert in the field of melanoma especially melanoma in children. She spent time with me explaining my condition in great detail. Larry was with me. I asked her if anyone in the world had a nevus as large as mine. She said, "Yes, there is a young lady from Ireland that has one just as large as yours, maybe a little larger." She told me that it covered the girl's entire chest and neck. I almost did not believe her because I thought surely no one could have a birthmark as large as mine. But I *did* believe her. I asked her about what the Connecticut dermatologist had said. She said that it was unfortunate that I had to experience that type of behavior from a physician and that he was wrong. She said the largest threat of developing melanoma is in childhood. The second largest threat was during pregnancy. The third was menopause, and it was more like a 5 percent chance. Recent studies show that it is more like 2 percent. She made my day. I was to see her every six months for a checkup which gave Larry and I a chance to tour different parts of Glasgow with each visit.

Today, as I write, I am saddened by discovering that another young innocent life (age three) has been lost to nevus-related melanoma. We must find a cure for this hideous form of cancer and also giant congenital nevus.

About six months after the first meeting with her, I noticed a hard nodule on the lower right side of my back just a few inches under my waist. Larry said we should let Professor Mackie examine it, so we made an appointment, and off to Glasgow we went.

She looked at it and said, "I'm sure that it is probably nothing, but we should remove it since you have never had a biopsy of your nevus." That is what I decided to do. I was extremely frightened. So along came the day, and we got in the car and drove it onto the ferry that led us to the highway and the trek to Glasgow University Hospital. I was never so scared in all my life. I said a little breath prayer over and over. "Lord, with your help, I will overcome this challenge." I said it about a hundred times. You see, there was a needle involved; needles and cancer are two of the most terrifying words in the English language to me.

We arrived at the Glasgow Infirmary (that is what they used to call it); it was, on that day, an extremely large creepy building. We checked in, and I was led to a waiting area. Then they walked me to the surgeon who had me lie down on a table. They apparently don't put patients in hospital gowns, at least not back then. I had a local anesthetic and felt a lot of pressure and then the tug, tug, of the stitches, and the little hard knot was gone. I was told to go back to the waiting area. I walked out and made the journey across the hospital and down a flight of stairs all by myself. I found a very relieved Larry waiting for me. I don't understand why they didn't let him come with me; it's a miracle I made it back to him without passing out. They gave me no pain meds; however, I found out from my Scottish friends that you could simply go to the pharmacy and get codeine pills, no prescription, so Larry did.

The stitches were painful in the paper-thin nevus skin, and it took forever to heal. The results didn't come back for several weeks. I remember when the postman put the letter through the door. I was terrified to open it, but I did really quickly, so fast that I almost ripped it in half. The test showed that it was totally benign. It was a happy day. That part of my back is still very sensitive.

I did not realize at the time, but meeting Professor Mackie was like meeting with a celebrity in the world of medicine. She is a spectacular physician. She was born in Dundee, Scotland. Her father was a professor of biochemistry at the University of Glasgow. She was educated at schools in Aberdeen, London, and Glasgow. This was followed by study at the university as holder of the Oliphant Bursary in Medicine and in 1970 was awarded the degree of MD with honors. She was an honorary clinical lecturer and became a professor of dermatology in 1978. The British Association of Dermatologists awarded her the Sir Archibald Grey Gold Medal in 1999.

Professor Mackie wrote many articles on melanoma; one was for *The British Journal of Dermatology* entitled "The Number and Distribution of Benign Pigmented Moles in Melanocytic Naevi." She is one of the most interesting people that I have ever met.

Our second and final American visitor was my niece, Tanya Balog, who visited us in 1988. She was in college at the time, and she was a true beauty (still is). We subjected her to a lot of boring things, so when she asked Larry and I to take her to a club, we had to say yes, although we did not want to. The club that was located in a complex over by the ship had a notorious reputation. So off we went to the enlisted men's club, and Tanya was stunning; I wanted to dress her in a burlap sack.

I prayed all evening that none of the sailors would flirt or whistle because Larry would have knocked them out. There were rules for Tanya set by me, and here they are starting with rule number one.

1. No dancing with drunks.
2. Dancing was to be done within plain sight of Larry and I, and I mean like not more than five feet away.
3. No dirty dancing; in other words, no touching.
4. No drinking for her (maybe one). She may have broken that rule (can't be sure).
5. No going to the ladies' room without *me*.
6. We leave at midnight.

The most important rule was not going to the bathroom without me. Sailors hung out by the ladies room. The night went well, and everyone had fun, even me.

We wanted Tanya to have the full Scottish experience, so we took her to get fish and chips. *Real* fish and chips served in newspaper and topped with vinegar. It's the best in the entire world. But, I think, the first actual trip we made with Tanya was the most exciting trip in the whole wide world for *me*, Loch Ness. Loch Ness is a large, deep, freshwater loch in the Scottish Highlands extending for approximately twenty-three miles southwest of Inverness and is home of the legendary Loch Ness Monster. I have wanted to visit Loch Ness ever since I was six years old and saw the famous picture of Nessie in a book. The present ruins date from the thirteenth to the sixteenth centuries, though built on the site of an early medieval fortification. In the twentieth century, it was placed in state care and opened to the public: it is now one of the most-visited castles in Scotland.

I was still recovering from my nevus biopsy when we took the journey to Loch Ness, but I was determined to go. The castle, overlooking Loch Ness, was one of the largest in Scotland (in area). It was defended by a ditch and drawbridge. The buildings of the castle were laid out around two main enclosures on the shore. Not much of it remains now; it is a ruin, but that is what gives it such a mysterious character. I was not happy to see the one million stone steps leading down to the castle. I took them very slowly, and it took forever to get back up to the car park, but I still enjoyed every minute of it. We had lunch at the Loch Ness Exhibition Centre, and, no, I did not spell center wrong. Centre is the correct spelling in Great Britain. The exhibition weighs the evidence of legend, psychology, and the environment. It also includes a number of important scientific findings but in words that everybody can understand. It is not just a monster exhibition. It tells people about Loch Ness and also about Scotland and the ecology of a Scottish loch. While the scientific discoveries are themselves fascinating, they also act as evidence in the great monster legend. No, we did not spot any monsters that day, but Tanya did get carsick on the way back!

We also took Tanya to Edinburgh to see Holyrood. Founded as a monastery in 1128, the Palace of Holyrood house in Edinburgh is the queen's official residence in Scotland. Holyrood house is closely associated with Scotland's turbulent past, including Mary, Queen of Scots, who lived here between 1561 and 1567. Successive kings and queens have made the Palace of Holyrood house the premier royal residence in Scotland. We had a wonderful time and a history lesson. When the day to venture over to Glasgow came about, I was just too tired to go, and my birthmark was making me uncomfortable. I was not fully healed and was exhausted from the Loch Ness trip. I asked Larry to take Tanya. They didn't want to go without me, but I begged them to go. You can't come all the way to Scotland and not see Glasgow. Glasgow is the largest city in Scotland and the third largest in the United Kingdom. Glasgow grew from a small rural settlement on the River Clyde to become one of the largest seaports in Britain. It is a lovely, vibrant city and was one of my favorites to visit. Then Tanya had to fly back home, and Michael and I really wanted to go with her but not without Larry.

Larry, Michael, and I took many trips to Glasgow. Once, we visited Glasgow Cathedral, also called St Mungo's Cathedral. Its former status was the Roman Catholic mother church of the Arch Diocese of Glasgow. The current congregation is the Presbytery Church of Scotland. I was amazed by the people that were visiting that day. They were from several different countries, and I knew this because they were speaking several languages. I ventured over to a man to ask what time it was, and he said in German that he didn't speak English. Early in the year 1989, they opened a McDonalds in Glasgow. It was Scotland's first McDonalds. We went as soon as possible after it opened! The only thing that was different tasting about it was the ketchup, and you had to pay for the ketchup; it was ten pence apiece.

We also visited the town of Stirling. Stirling is the largest city in central Scotland. The city is clustered around a large fortress and medieval old town. Stirling castle is one of the largest and most important castles, both historically and architecturally, in Scotland. The castle sits atop Castle Hill and is surrounded on three sides by steep cliffs, giving it a strong defensive position. A few structures of the fourteenth-century remain. Mary, Queen of Scots, was crowned there in 1542. It is supposed to be Scotland's most haunted castle, but we did not see any ghosts that day.

One of the most exciting things we got to see while living in Scotland was the Gold of the Pharaohs exhibit that took place in Edinburgh. It was an exhibition of ancient Egyptian treasures from the royal tombs of Tanis. The exhibition ran in the Edinburgh Art Center from February to April in 1988. It displayed artifacts from as early as 1200 BC. They were on loan from the Cairo Museum with some items from the Louvre in Paris and the British Museum. The accidental discovery of the tombs at Tanis came just eleven years after the sensational Tutankhamen tomb was unearthed. The mask of Tutankhamen was on loan from the Cairo Museum; there were jewel-encrusted death masks, sarcophagi, and priceless relics acquired by tomb raiders on display. We waited for two hours in a line that stretched out forever. It was worth the wait.

While living in Scotland, Larry and I purchased a piano so that our son, Michael, could take lessons. As soon as we got back to the States, karate took the place of piano lessons. I thought about talking lessons, but when? I just never had time. We lugged that piano to three residences, and it was heavy. When they packed us out from Scotland, I watched eight Scottish guys lift this iron-framed upright Baldwin piano up in the air and into a wooden crate. They had no ramp, and I cringed as they groaned and most likely herniated. We sold that piano two years ago when we moved into our new house that we had built in 2012. It went to a great home. It was bought by a woman that collected antique instruments. We left Scotland in May of 1989, and while we were on the ferry for the last time, I looked back at the Holy Loch, and I was a little sad because I knew that I would never see it again.

I have wonderful memories of our Scotland adventure, but the three years we were there went by very slowly. They started talking about closing Site One in 1987, and I prayed that they would close it fast so that we could go home. In June of 1987, the Hunley was relieved by the Simon Lake. Larry still worked continuously night and day. We left Scotland and went back to Pennsylvania and then on to Virginia in 1989.

But they did not close the site until the Cold War came to an end with the demise of the Soviet Union. In March of 1992, the last US Navy ship, the submarine tender USS Simon Lake, sailed out of the Holy Loch, ending thirty-one years of American presence in the area.

Virginia

You'll always be
our great Virginia.
You're the heartland of the nation.
Where history
was changed forever.
Today, your glory stays,
as we build tomorrow.

—Mike Geenly, 2014

While we were living in Scotland, Larry received orders to Norfolk, Virginia. We were thrilled. Pennsylvania was an eight-hour drive and North Carolina only a four hour drive. The day finally came, and we were riding the ferry and on our way to the Glasgow airport just like we arrived three years before. We arrived back at Pittsburg International very thrilled to be back home in May of 1989. Michael and I stayed the summer with Larry's parents while he attended a school in California. Then he came back in November, and we made our way to Norfolk, Virginia.

When I visited Professor Mackie for the last time in Glasgow, she referred me to a Dr. Brian Jegasothy who was a professor of dermatology at the University of Pittsburgh School of Medicine. She wanted to have a really good dermatologist examine my birthmark from year to year to detect any changes that may occur. I only spoke with him on the phone, and he was a very nice man with genuine concern and interest. However, he suggested that I see another physician from Harvard whose research was in the area of giant congenital melanocytic nevus.

So I did. I know that Dr. Jegasothy thought he was doing a wonderful thing for me. But it was a huge mistake; I guess my clue should have been the word research.

As Larry was in California, his sister, Cathy, came with me to Pittsburgh to see the doctor from Harvard. Let's call him Dr. Harvard. I went in to see him alone while Cathy was waiting in the waiting room. Larry is always with me, so I was really nervous. So there I sat in my underwear with that little paper gown for what seemed like forever. In walked Dr. Harvard, and I could tell right away that he was all business. He did the exam and proceeded to tell me all the rhetoric that I have heard from physicians in the past, cancer, death, and he explained that they have a new way of removal. They insert the equivalent of water balloons under your good skin, chop out the bad skin, and then sew it all up nice and neat. I asked if there would be scarring; the answer was yes. I asked if he could remove every inch of my nevus; the answer was no. Could the nevus come back? The answer was yes. He was practically salivating to make me his science project, and I was not agreeing. So he did something no dermatologist has done before. He said, "I hope that you understand that your deformity *really* bothers your husband. I mean, it *has* to." How low can somebody go? It was the cruelest thing anyone has ever said to me. Then he said, "There are infants and small children over at the Children's Hospital of Pittsburgh having this surgery done all the time for various afflictions. So why are you being so immature about this?"

So I left; angry, sad, and everything in between. Needless to say, I never went back.

I should have seen Dr. Jegasothy instead. I was very sad to hear of his passing from Parkinson's disease and cancer at the age of fifty-eight. I read that his medical research was instrumental in finding a cure for CTCL (cutaneous T-cell lymphoma) which is a rare blood cancer which manifests itself in the skin. It is this type of research that will ultimately cure most skin cancers and chronic skin disease.

So off to Norfolk, Virginia, we went in November of 1989, and we have been here ever since. I remember the first time we came out of the Hampton tunnel and could see the naval base to the right. I said to Larry, "I think that we are really going to like it here." We liked it enough to retire in the Virginia Beach/Chesapeake area. I was a stay at home mom ever since Michael was born. Michael was eight years old when we arrived in Virginia Beach and moved into our apartment. All three of us were dealing with the culture shock of going from peaceful and serene Scotland to hustle and bustle, traffic, eight-lane highways, and not to mention it being populous. There were a half million people living in Virginia Beach alone. We bought our first home in 1990. It was a townhome in a wonderful school district. We lived there for seven years and then purchased a brick ranch where we lived for fifteen years. Then in 2012, we purchased our current home.

One day, in early 1990, I found the weirdest hive-like itchy bump on my tummy (non-birthmark skin). I thought nothing of it until I woke up the next day with my tummy covered in these little itchy pumps. So off to the dermatologist I went. He told me that it was pityriasis rosea. The exact cause is not known, but it may be from a virus. This condition is not contagious, and no one in my family caught it from me. There is really no treatment, except for the itching. As with chicken pox and measles, pityriasis rosea only appeared on my non-birthmark skin. It was very uncomfortable, and it lasted six weeks. The rash covered my neck but did not spread to my face. The rash slowly faded away and did not scar. I wonder how many of my nevus friends have had this?

Another thing totally unrelated to nevus sent me to the dermatologist while living in our townhome. I woke up one morning, and the bottom of my left arm was swollen twice its size. Larry was on deployment, of course, so I showed it to a neighbor saying, "Do you think I should be concerned about this?" I heard "yikes" as they jumped back, and so I took that as a yes and went to the doctor.

Dr. Oppenheim looked at me and said, "Oh, yes, this is a brown recluse spider bite, but don't worry, you won't die from it because you would be dead by now. Here is a cream for the itching." So I went on a spider hunt when I got home and guess where I found it, under the arm of a folding lawn chair that I sat in outside while reading. I gleefully murdered a spider that day. I have a huge distain for spiders.

1998 Nevus Outreach

What would you think if I sang out of tune
Would you stand up and walk out on me?
Lend me your ears and I'll sing you a song
And I'll try not to sing out of key
Oh, I get by with a little help from my friends
Mm I get high with a little help from my friends
Mm going to try with a little help from my friends.
—The Beatles, 1967)

Sometime during the winter of 1998, I was on the computer, working. Out of nowhere came a thought. Wonder what would happen if I typed the word nevus into the internet. So I did and up came Nevus Outreach. That is when I became e-mail pals with Kathryn Rose Stewart whose daughter, Megan, was born with a nevus almost identical to mine. At the time, Megan was about two years old, and now she is a beautiful young lady. It meant the world to me that Kathryn spent so much time on e-mail with me. Megan was the first person I knew of with a birthmark as large as mine. I was shocked, I was comforted, I was sad, and I was happy, and then came the waterfall of tears that I was really not alone.

Kathryn's husband, Mark Beckwith, was at one time the executive director of Nevus Outreach. He has devoted his life to promoting the mission, promoting awareness, providing support, and finding a cure. Kathy and Mark are two of the six cofounders of Nevus Outreach founded in 1997.

Way back then, there was no Facebook, but there was e-mail. There was a way of communicating through the Nevus Outreach website. I remember in those early days getting an e-mail from a father of an infant daughter with a giant nevus. He was from South America, Bolivia, I think. Anyway, he was asking me about my life, how I grew up, my self-esteem, any problems, any surgeries, etc. He asked me every conceivable question, and I was very happy to answer. He asked if I was ever upset with my parents for not removing my nevus when I was a baby. I answered that I was elated that my parents did not put me through such an ordeal. He talked about bringing his little girl to the United States for removal. I really didn't know how to answer. You see, it is such a personal decision.

Nevus Outreach sponsors a conference every few years where nevus families, physicians, and speakers gather from all across the globe. I have never been to a conference, but I hope to go in the future. Nevus wearers and their families travel from Australia, India, New Zealand, South Africa, the Middle East, France, Germany, Norway, Poland, Sweden, Switzerland, the Netherlands, the United Kingdom, Argentina, Brazil, Canada, Columbia, Mexico, and many other countries *and* from across the United States. They are mainly held in Texas, so Larry and I will have to drive. I don't do airplanes anymore.

A great deal of progress has been made in organizing and sharing knowledge among interdisciplinary scientists worldwide. These scientists now work together as part of the Nevus Outreach extended family, accumulating data, testing theories in pursuit of a cure, and caring for families affected by nevi. They travel from Brazil, France, Germany, Mexico City, Switzerland, and across the United States to join families at the nevus conferences to share what they are learning with one another.

Parents attended a number of sessions intended to help them best manage their child's nevi and related conditions. Whether or not to remove a nevus is a personal choice and is not right for everyone for many reasons. For families considering this option, however, physicians described the tissue expansion/nevus removal surgery favored in the United States and those procedures commonly practiced in other countries. Similar sessions were devoted to skin care and cosmetics and how to help a child respond to the psychological challenges of having a nevus. There are also enjoyable events to attend like the talent show, the dinner and dance, and many other things.

Children and teens go on a variety of field trips such as Sea Life Aquarium, Six Flags, the movies, and the mall. Then they head to the pool, where the word is that a number of girls wore bikinis for the very first time. A number of "Nevus Life" sessions were focused on kids from eight to twelve and teens, thirteen to seventeen, to talk about the special challenges they face as children with nevi, and siblings of children with nevi.

There is a Nevus Outreach page on Facebook, and there is another page just for nevus adults. I have joined both. The main Nevus Outreach Facebook page is for everyone to share stories and news about research, etc. It's mostly comprised of parents of children with birthmarks. We old folk nevus people share our stories with them and try to help them in any way that we can. The nevus adult page is just for, well, nevus adults. Now that Facebook can translate just about any language to English, we can communicate with other giant birthmark wearers from all over the world. It's awesome. We share problems and stories, and although we all have the same nevus, we are all so profoundly unique. *We* are some interesting people!

Although it is heartbreaking to hear of a fellow nevus wearer diagnosed with melanoma, most of them win their fight if caught early. We fellow nevites keep in touch, share information, and cheer them on. On the other side of the coin, we feel so very, very, very sad when they lose their battle. When you really think about it, life is that way for everyone. We are born, we live our life, however short or long, we find a way to deal with what life gives us, and then we depart this life and go to the Lord. It's what we do with the time we are given here on Earth that matters.

The Nevus Outreach website is more than just a website. It contains the Nevus Outreach Registry; this is an international registry of large congenital melanocytic nevi and related melanosis, is the only registry of its kind for large nevi, and provides a growing source of statistical information about this rare condition. It's a very important mission, and the hope is that the information gathered will lead to a better understanding of large nevi, provide this information to physicians, and possibly find better treatments.

The initial analysis of the Nevus Outreach Registry (which I am proud to be a part of) resulted in important findings, which have helped physicians understand large nevi better. This confidential data has been the basis of numerous peer-reviewed medical publications. The statistical information in the registry will provide the basis for a better understanding of large nevi and related disorders that could lead to improved treatments, prevention, awareness, and a cure!

Nevus Outreach, Inc., is dedicated to bringing awareness, providing support, and finding cures for people affected by congenital melanocytic nevi (CMN) and related disorders. Your gift is vital to transforming the lives of people with this condition.

You may make a tax-deductible donation today or become an Outreach Angel by making a commitment to give monthly or quarterly.

Contact Nevus Outreach today for more information at:
Nevus Outreach, Inc.
600 SE Delaware Ave., Suite 200
Bartlesville, OK 74003
918-331-0595
www.nevus.org

Our Thirty-Fifth Wedding Anniversary

Did you know that before you came into my life
It was some kind of miracle that I survived
Some day we will both look back
And have to laugh
We lived through a lifetime
And the aftermath

This is the time to remember
Cause it will not last forever
These are the days
To hold on to
Cause we won't
Although we want to
And so we embrace again
Behind the dunes
This beach is cold
On winter afternoons
But holding you close is like holding the summer sun
I'm warm from the memory of days to come.
—(Billy Joel, 1986)

When Larry asked me to marry him, he promised that he would never leave me or make me cry and that we would have a wonderful happy life together. He has kept that promise. We are best friends and business partners. Life is not without its share of problems, and Larry is an excellent problem solver. There is nothing that the two of us can't figure out together. He is kind, generous, gentle, and loving and has always encouraged me to be the very best person that I could be. Being married to him has made me be a better person, and knowing him has given me the ability to gain a huge amount of self-esteem. He has helped me to overcome shyness and insecurities. All that I am today (award-winning Realtor, business partner, mother, grandmother, and author), I owe to my husband Larry's continued advice, guidance, kind words, and constant love. He is a fantastic father and grandfather. He is extremely intelligent and has a great sense of humor. I can be having a bad day, and in ten seconds, he can have me laughing. He is hardworking and basically sacrificed his life to the military so that Michael and I could have a better life. He had an amazing naval career, and I could not be more proud of him.

I remember having a whiney day and saying to him, "Why couldn't I have won the lottery instead of receiving this awful birthmark?"

I'll never forget this. He said, "I won the lottery the day that I met you."

As I write this, Larry and I have just returned home from visiting the serene and majestic mountains of Charlottesville, Virginia, to celebrate our thirty-fifth wedding anniversary. We had an amazing trip, but it went by way too fast. The weather was absolutely perfect, seventy-eight degrees, bright and sunny with a few big puffy clouds floating by in a light breeze. You know that we are *really* into houses because we sell real estate, and we are very interested in history. Larry and I could not wait to see Monticello (in Italian means little mountain), the home of Thomas Jefferson. Jefferson was our third president, one of our nation's founding fathers, and principal writer of the Declaration of Independence. It sits on the summit of an 850-foot peak, and the views are spectacular. He designed much of it himself and used as a guide elements popular in late eighteenth-century Europe. It was a working plantation that he started building when he was twenty-six years old. He inherited five thousand acres of land from his father. He mostly grew tobacco. Monticello has been designated a National Historic Landmark.

Weakened by childbirth, Thomas Jefferson's wife, Martha, died a few months after the birth of her sixth child from excessive bleeding. Only two of their children lived to adulthood, and only one got past the age of twenty-five. When Jefferson died, he was buried on the grounds in what is now a family graveyard in which Thomas Jefferson's descendants are buried. I was so excited to see it, but when we got there, the entire cemetery, which was actually quite small, was surrounded by a huge black wrought iron fence. So I was the tiniest bit disappointed to not be able to roam around in the graveyard and read the tombstones.

Life at Monticello was full of challenges. For me, growing up as a person living with a GNC, which is packed with emotional and physical challenges, it was about finding the right perspective when it came to the big picture of my life and what I wanted to do with it. I was always hard on myself especially when things did not go my way, but just like that little train (I think I can, I think I can, I think I can), I repeatedly told myself that I had the power to do it, and I became a glowing optimist. The power of positive thinking has brought me through many of life's inevitable rough times.

The day we arrived in Charlottesville, we went directly to the historic downtown area where there are great restaurants, shops, and street performers. We had dinner there and did some shopping. What astonished me about Charlottesville was the amount of homeless people. It broke my heart. They are on every corner with their cardboard signs pleading for help. My mom always said that if someone asks you for spare change or something to eat, you should help them. There were a lot of them, so we could not give to all. There are a lot worse things in life than living with a giant congenital birthmark.

We spent our first full day at Monticello and had dinner at the Michie Tavern, a Virginia Historic Landmark. It was southern cookin' fried chicken, biscuits, black-eyed peas, and on and on; the food was fabulous and so was the view from our table, the magnificent mountains. Larry and I felt right at home there since we both grew up at the foot of the mountain in southwestern Pennsylvania. We went searching for antiques, enjoyed wonderful food, and also visited James Madison's Montpelier. It was the perfect way to celebrate thirty-five years of marriage. We had an amazing time that we will always remember. I framed a picture that I took of Monticello that day with the big puffy clouds and sunny day and hung it in our home office above Larry's desk.

Our twenty-fifth anniversary was spent at Disneyworld in Orlando, Florida, in September of 2004. We stayed an entire week at the Port Orleans Riverside Resort (our favorite). Our waterfront room at Port Orleans Magnolia Bend depicts the plantations of the old south and was spotless as was the entire resort. It has stately courtyards, charming fountains, and formal gardens recreating the opulence of the antebellum south. There are horse-drawn carriage rides, a formal restaurant, a not so formal restaurant, shops, a huge swimming pool, and many other amenities. Our favorite thing is the boat service that takes you on a splendid ride to Downtown Disney where we saw Cirque du Soleil La Nuba; it was mesmerizing.

We have been to Disney around ten or so times. I remember our very first trip in 1995. Michael was thirteen. The whole way down in the car, I was thinking why we are doing this; it's going to be a glorified Busch Gardens. I could not have been more wrong. The three of us had the time of our life. Because of my birthmark, I don't ride amusement rides; however, I could do almost everything at Disney except the roller coasters. You see, Disney is not an amusement park, it is a glorious fantasy that allows you to escape every conceivable worry, trouble, or problem you may have. Mr. Disney wanted to create a place where every member of the family could have fun, children, parents, and grandparents too. There are so many things to see and experience and learn, and the entire family can do them (most times) together.

The parks are magnificent, and we always do The Magic Kingdom first. No matter how many times we visit The Magic Kingdom, we are always amazed by its beauty. The first time I saw Cinderella Castle, it took my breath away. It is much larger than it looks on television, and every night after the fireworks or spectro magic parade, Tinker Bell flies from the top spire of the castle all the way to Tomorrow Land and disappears. Our favorite things at The Magic Kingdom are Pirates of the Caribbean, The Jungle Cruise, The Enchanted Tiki Room, Liberty Belle Riverboat, The Hall of Presidents, The Haunted Mansion, It's a Small World, Winnie the

Pooh, The Carousel of Progress, Peter Pan's flight, the numerous shows, and much more.

At Epcot, they had an entire pavilion dedicated to video games and technology in 1995. Michael would have stayed there all day if we had let him. My favorite Epcot attraction now is called Soarin'. It is a hand glider simulator, and it really feels like you are hand gliding. We also like Spaceship Earth which is a huge, pardon the pun, golf ball that greets you as you enter the park. Yes, it is a ride; it's very slow and takes you high inside the seventeen-story geosphere that takes you through the history of communication from cave drawings to computers. There is also the Animal Kingdom and Hollywood Studios. There is a fifth park rumored to be built within the next few years. Fair warning to those of you with very young children, children age four and under do not do well because of all the over-stimulation. Many times, Larry and I see parents with toddlers and infants, and believe me when I say that everyone in their troop is usually quite miserable. There is a lot of wailing and crying, and that is just from the parents.

If you have a child with a giant congenital nevus or any other disability, you must take them to Disney if you get the chance. It truly is the happiest place on Earth. It's the one place that Larry and I can truly relax. There are no birthmarks at Disney.

Through the years, we have been on fabulous adventures together, and I look forward to hopefully many more as the Lord allows.

Stuff Larry's Mom Said

Parts of your life can be comical, if you
let it, even with a birthmark.

Larry's mom, my mother-in-law, passed away in the summer of 2013. She lived in rural Pennsylvania her entire life. She was as strong as an ox and lived on her own in a house that she referred to as her little structure. We all called her Nan. As long as I have known her, she has said the funniest things. Here are a few of the quotes I have gathered throughout the years. Nan talked nonstop twenty-four hours a day, seven days a week, and almost every single thing she said was either comical, witty, or interesting; sometimes it's all three. I started writing down all the eccentric things that she said because let's face it, they *are* pretty funny. When she found out about my birthmark after the birth of my son, she said to me. "That's OK, Lori, my friend was born with one eye in the middle of her forehead. They fixed it, and now she can see just fine."

Here are some other quotes:

"I once knew this man who would come into a room and talk and talk and talk. Nobody would listen, but he just talked and talked. They found out that his brain was in sideways."

One day, during the summer, when Larry was at work and Michael was out with his friends, I decided to take Nan to the beach to have lunch even though when I asked her about it, she said, "Seagulls scare me, but I'll go as long as you feed me." It's about a twenty-minute drive from our house. Larry and I are both Realtors, so I was doing some last-minute computer work before making the lunch trip. Nan was studying me while I was working. Then she stated, "The computer is from the devil." Then she performed the sign of the cross and left the room muttering, "If I had to type like that, I'd go crazy and be in prison."

We made it into the car, and Nan comments about the local real estate offices. "All of these real estate offices are in the same place as yours. That's too much compensation for you. I could have never been a real estate agent because I have paranoia."

We finally arrived at the beach front, and Nan suddenly exclaimed, "Look, Lori, those hotels have jacooties!" A few minutes later. "Am I getting a tan, or is this jaundice?" We arrived at the seaside restaurant overlooking the ocean, and we actually had a nice meal. Afterward, we sat at a bench on the boardwalk watching the beach people go by: some jogging, some on rollerblades, some on bicycles because it was a beautiful day. Larry's mom said to me, "This boardwalk is full of odd people. Look at all the incest up here." Nan (back then) loved her cigarettes; she gazed at me with the saddest look on her face and said, "It's so hot out here I can hardly smoke." Followed by, "Let's go get slip slops and walk on the beach."

Speaking about her days as a nurse, "I felt bad for the dead people I had to put in body bags, so I always poked a little hole in the bag so they could breathe."

While visiting us in Virginia Beach, "There is never any dust in Lori's house. The ocean must clean it out because Lori never dusts."

On employment, "That guy just talks and talks and talks. I don't know what he's talking about, but at least he works."

Seagull comment, "There has to be a God because the birds know not to fly high up where there is no air."

At Christmas, Nan liked to walk around munching on cookies. We find bits and pieces of cookie absolutely everywhere you can imagine. Naturally, we try to clean up after her. Larry had to go around with a handheld vacuum cleaner to pick up all the crumbs. This quote came from Larry's sister when she picked Nan up from the airport after spending Christmas with us. It goes like this. "It's amazing how organized Lori and Larry are, and they're so clean. They have to clean up every little speck of dirt they see, even the dirt they don't see. They even have a special sweeper to pick up the lint on the carpet that you can't even see. Larry runs it all day long."

While dining out, "I don't like to go out and eat with what's her name. She talks too much and says stupid things."

"That squirrel in Larry and Lori's front yard is nuts."

"There are no homeless people in this city. It's so clean. The police must hurry and take them away in big trucks."

"I have no more bugs around my house since they spread all that spermacide around."

"I don't know why Christmas and Thanksgiving are so close together, but it explains it in the Bible."

A compliment. "I like your coat, Lori. Those old worn-out coats are back in style."

During the holiday season, the second we walked through the front door. "Larry, do you have a Christmas card that I could use to give to Phillip?"

"Yes, Mom, I'll get it for you in a minute."

Two seconds later, "Mike, do you have a Christmas card I could use to give to Phillip?"

"Yes, Nan, Mom has some, and I'll get one for you in a minute."

Two more seconds later (we didn't even have our coats off yet), "Larry, do you have a Christmas card I could use to give to Phillip?"

Finally, I couldn't take it anymore, I put down what I was carrying and hurried to get a card from my home office and handed her the much-needed Christmas card.

She looks at me and says, "What is this for?"

My nephew once decided to ask Nan the long-debated question about whether she thought the glass was half empty or half full while pouring her a soft drink. Her response was, "That's enough."

While she was visiting with my brother-in-law, Nan was wearing a small red ruby slippers pin. He thought it had something to do with the Wizard of Oz. When he made a comment about it, she said, "These red slippers belonged to Jesus."

At Sunday dinners and Christmas dinner, we usually will have the youngest person at the table read a passage from the Bible. One Christmas dinner (which we always have on Christmas Eve), Nan said after the reading, "These people that write Bibles, they all write different stories. You have to pick the one you understand." We all smiled and continued to eat by candlelight; Nat King Cole was singing "O Holy Night," and everything was quiet and serene, but that lasted for just an instant. Then Nan with a puzzled look on her face puts down her fork, stops eating and asks, "What happens in the Bible on Christmas Eve?"

I excused myself from the table for a moment to return to her saying, "I once watched porno. It was an accident. It was the highlight of my year." You just never know what she will say next. The year before, at the Christmas dinner table, she shared this with Larry, Michael, and I. "I don't know what I am still doing here when everybody I ever loved is dead and gone."

Out of nowhere, "If you bring an owl into your house, you will suddenly die. But I can't prove that."

On the holidays, "It's difficult to be old and nice at the same time, well after all, that is what Christmas is all about...money."

While riding in the car, "I once saw a married couple with eight or nine children, and the children were all of different species."

On patriotism, "It's a free country, but it's best to keep your mouth shut."

"Can I touch them?" After a friend's breast enhancement surgery.

On geography, "Your people in India die in such large numbers that they just throw them in the Nile."

On gift giving, "It was so vitally important for me to buy this gift for what's his name."

On science, "Grapefruits don't have all those seeds like they used to. They breed them different now."

Neighborhood advice, "People who live in small villages should ignore stupid village people talk."

On medicine, "Tennerum is that pill they use for ten different things."

On religion, "I'm not going to church anymore. Only sick people go to church."

On housework, "I've been doing laundry all day and trying to organize my doors."

On air travel, "Did you know that J.F.K. Jr. died in one of those stupid planes you put together yourself?"

On air travel, "People should not fly today and carry anything metallic. That's why I put my money in my bra."

On air travel, "They nearly stripped searched me on the plane from Arizona, and that was before 7-11."

On foreign travel, "Larry, please don't think about going to other countries because Russia is full of TB. They don't have the medicine needed, and the prisoners are full of TB. Hawaii is also full of volcanoes, but that's none of my business."

While riding in the car, "See those white cows over there? It's not normal for cows to be white. This means they are evil. They pop up out of evil holes in the ground. Never drink milk from a white cow."

On meteorology, "Did you know that every time they shoot something up into space the weather all over the world goes haywire?"

On health and aging, "I had an MRI on that eye that was bleeding."

"I think my hearing aid went deaf"

"When you turn eighty, your whole body collapses."

"Did you ever get a headache in your eye?"

"When you get old, all your fingernails fall off."

"See how your mind gets crazy when you're old?"

"I can't stand old people. They drive you nuts because they can't move their hands."

Said out of the blue, "When you set your hummingbird loose, it takes a long time for them to get their head together."

On southern history, "The Klan was nothing more than a bunch of hillbillies that went insane."

About technology, "They have eliminated videos. All they have now is VD" (meaning DVDs).

What really gives you ulcers. "You know that's what gives you ulcers? The flies that come in on the fruit from Africa, my doctor said so."

On Lori's cooking, "Lori's food tastes good because there is no soot in the air. Your homemade spaghetti is good, Lori. Larry always did like his food bland with no taste."

About birth control, "I got pregnant all the time because I couldn't use an IUD like Aunt Edith."

"My watch is a Bolivia." While staring at her watch.

Facts about Ireland. "You know, there are still elves in Ireland."

On fine dining, "Wonder what cornish hens taste like?"

"Blonds look better with gray in their hair. Look at how pretty Cathy's hair looks?" (Cathy has jet black hair.)

When she broke her dentures, "Somebody put a curse on my teeth."

Comments about eyesight:

- "They have all kinds of technicians for macular degeneration."
- "I need an eye transplant."
- "I have to be and will continue to be obsessed with my eyes."
- "Macular degeneration is a deadly disease."
- "Sonya is losing her mind because she can't hear out of her left eye".
- "I'm deaf in this one eye."
- "Men who take Viagra go blind."

(On a side note, some of the medically proven side effects of Viagra are blurred, abnormal, or double vision, vision changes, or temporary blindness. This a written in the rare side effects of Viagra from Drugs.com viewed June 29, 2014.)

Hometown fact. "Fayette County is the most des-ta-lute county in Pennsylvania."

On vices, "Lori, staying at your house is better than gambling."

When Larry retired from twenty years of serving with the US Navy, "Sex, sex, sex, why is everything on TV always talking about sex? Maybe that is why Larry is sad about retirement. You should feed him Viagra."

On agriculture, "Heroine is the top agricultural product. They put it in pipes and make little boys smoke it."

On Catholicism:

- "I say my rosary every night. It's the same thing as counting sheep. It helps me fall asleep."
- "When I say my rosary, I have to concentrate on my toes."
- "I went with Cathy to Uniontown to the Church of Saint Paul of Whatever."
- "They are so cheap at church they made the wafers that you get at the altar really small."
- "God punishes you when you say bad things."

On roadways, "Lori, do younz have Penn Dot down here?"

Nan words, "Uniontown has all new restaurants like Ruby Tuesday and ISOP."

From our nephew, he was complaining about his back bothering him, and Nan told him to "get one on those vibrators like Uncle Larry uses on Aunt Lori."

On geography and voodoo, "You know voodoo is very active in the south especially in Oregon."

At the airport, "There were only six normal people on my flight, and I was one of them."

Nan speaking on Hitler. "How could that little shit even have that position?"

Larry said to Nan, "Why do you think I hate you, Mom?"

She answered, "Because I had your sisters."

On country music, "I like to listen to Wille Nillie" (Willie Nelson).

On entertainment, "Are you talking about Meryl Lynch, the movie star?" (Meryl Streep).

Just after being introduced to the family next door, "I knew a family that had really big heads, and their bodies were really little."

On her children, "My oldest son is very handsome but not as beautiful as my Larry."

On vacationing, "I don't like the ocean at Aruba. I only like the ocean at the Bahamas."

While visiting Pennsylvania, "Larry, we have to go to Vestaburg to get that painting. It is vitally important that we go tomorrow. If we don't go tomorrow to pick up the painting, it would be very bad."

Larry says, "OK, Mom, we will go tomorrow."

Nan replies, "Go where, son?"

While reading a friend's obituary, "They forgot to write that he was insane."

On telling the truth, "I didn't tell him that Larry. I didn't tell him anything at all. I did not tell him. Wait, I did tell him."

"My grandson started a ball thing where he lives. Now he has everyone doing it!" Nan's grandson loves baseball.

Nan mentioned that this was her second husband's marriage proposal. 'We just have to get married. Please marry me. Let's get married, and I'm having lots of prostate surgery so you won't have to worry about that."

A conversation about teaching. "What's his name is dating a teacher whose a nurse."

About her heritage, "My mother didn't like me because I was Irish."

High school memories. "I was a majorette, but I had no boots."

At church, the person in front of us was walking with a cane. "I could never walk with a cane. I'd fall down."

While watching the evening news, "This world is too evil, even for kids."

While driving past tall buildings, "Tall buildings scare me. I'd hate to be working in one of those tall buildings after 7-11 happened in Pittsburgh."

World events, "Morocco is a Greek island where that king got killed after he married an American."

It's a beautiful day in the neighborhood. "I never dreamed my neighborhood would have a prostitution house."

Just think, it all began with Mario, Luigi, and Duck Hunt. "Nintendo makes you smart, that's why they teach it in public schools now."

"I knew this guy. He was a little slow because he was in the military." Hmmmm

"Computers are going to be the destruction of the world." She may have a point with this one.

Nan came into the room holding up her dentures which were stored in one of my good Tupperware containers, saying with a gummy smile, "Lori, can I keep this to store my teeth in?"

Poor Evelyn. "Evelyn still has her own teeth, but they look so horrible."

On dentistry, "I want teeth implants, the kind they do with a laser beam."

Sense and sensibility, "That guy is a complete idiot, but he makes perfect sense."

On emotions, "Anger makes me really hungry."

While getting dressed in the morning, "Underwear confuses me."

Love is blind. "That lady up the street is blind, but she can see good enough to have sex with my next-door neighbor."

While visiting Pennsylvania, Larry had this discussion with his mom. "Mom, you are very healthy. You will probably out live all of your children."

She replied, "Oh, son," slight pause, "I sure hope so."

Adventures in Real Estate

In 1996, when Larry was promoted to Chief Petty Officer in the Navy, he decided to get his real estate license. We were thinking about selling our townhome and buying a single-family home, and he wanted to know exactly what that entailed. I thought he had lost his mind. I thought, *Why in the world would he want to do this when he was already so busy.* He explained that he had always had an interest in real estate, and it may be a good career choice after retirement from the military. So he went on to real estate school. Then he listed our house and sold it, he listed the neighbor's house and sold it, other people wanted him to sell their house, *then* he asked me to quit my job and go into real estate, crickets, chirp, chirp.

I was working at the Lillian Vernon Corporation in the QCH department, quality call handling. I had worked for years taking catalogue orders, and I applied for a seasonal QCH position, and I got it. I *loved* it. I did not want to go into real estate; I hate math.

I said to Larry, "I hate math, meaning, I am not good at math and therefore despise it."

He said, "There is not much math involved, in fact hardly any."

I did not want to become a Realtor because I was afraid that I would not be smart enough to pass the state exam. Larry encouraged me to try. It's easy for someone to look at the abilities they lack and then start to feel bad that they don't know enough or can't do enough.

But by shifting the focus to your long list of abilities and all of the things you can do, you start getting inspired rather than discouraged, and more things start to go your way. You'll start playing to your strengths instead of wallowing in your weaknesses. I did. I love my career now, and I am very good at it. I have just earned my fourteenth consecutive Circle of Excellence Award from the Hampton

Roads Realtor Association. I am an Accredited Buyer Representative (ABR). I am a Graduate of Real Estate Institute (GRI), and I have my Military Relocation Professional (MRP). Larry is an Associate Broker, CRS, GRI, e-Pro, MRP, and he has a Bachelor of Arts degree in Business Administration from California University of Pennsylvania. Larry and I go to work every day with enthusiasm, and we are passionate about real estate and helping people achieve the American dream.

Through the years, we have sold houses by the ocean, houses across the tunnel in Gloucester, small houses, huge houses, condos, townhomes, a house that sat on concrete blocks for a foundation, a condemned house, bank-owned homes, luxury homes, horse farms, you name it. We have been in real estate for over twenty-two years now, and we have met a lot of great people. We have made a lot of friends here in Virginia through the past thirty years, and only one friend of mine knows about my nevus.

This chapter is not birthmark related. However, some of the things that have happened to us as Realtors are pretty out of the ordinary. If it is a rare occurrence, it has probably happened to us. Larry and I have had many adventures in real estate, and I would like to share some of them with you. The first one I'd like to call...

To Bee or Not to Bee

Many years ago, on one of our numerous Disney vacations, Larry answered his phone; he many times does on vacation. The call was from a young lady that was in the Navy and was about to deploy. She did not want to put a tenant in her home while she was gone; she wanted us to just check on it once a week for six months. We agreed to watch her house for her while it was empty for $100 a month and water her plants. Why not, right? No tenants to watch over, so what could go wrong? Well the first week we went over to check on things, the house had a terrible stench. The source of which was a refrigerator full of rotted food. So we had to go out and get masks, gloves, and garbage bags and empty the entire contents of a full refrigerator and take it to the dumpster. Then we had the joyous task of scrubbing out the said stinky refrigerator. The next week, we discovered that the house was full of tiny little nasty flying gnats which I think somehow were related to the stinky food but were not there originally. We had to spray the house with bug spray. A few weeks passed, and then we walked in the door to find the security system beeping, so we changed the batteries, didn't fix it. We had to call the security company. That malfunction caused Larry to have to sit in an empty house for five solid hours because they could not give us an exact time to come out and fix it. *Then* there was a water leak and stain, while the handyman was there working he utilized the patio for his workspace.

He calls me and says, "Lori, I'm out here on the patio, and bees keep pelting me and flying away. I went out to the yard to investigate and that big half-rotted tree has tons of bees living in it."

OK, so we had to call an exterminator and meet him at the house.

The exterminator says, "I can't kill these bees. They are honeybees, and they are protected."

OK, g-r-e-a-t, so we called a beekeeper, and he tells us that we have to call someone to take down the tree because when he takes the bees, the queen will come right back to that tree unless we take it down. *Terrific.* So we scheduled the beekeeper and the tree people for the same day. On that day, we went over to the house to check on the beekeeper. It was a cool misty morning, and we find the beekeeper on a ladder tethered with ropes swinging a chainsaw in one hand and bees flying all around him. It was like something out of a movie. He was hacking down the tree as he took the bees. He saw us from far away and yells, "Hey, Porters, no need for the tree guys. I got this. It's a perfect day for beekeepin' and this is a premo hive. Wooh!"

So we backed out of the yard and let him do his thing. So several hundred dollars later, the bees and the tree were gone. I think that all in all, we had about seven hundred dollars wrapped up in that house on repairs that we paid out of our own pocket. When the owner came back home, she paid us back and was so happy with the work that we did for her; she allowed us to sell that home, and she and her boyfriend bought a house together from us, and when they left the area, we sold that house, and we got both sides of the commission because we brought the buyer and then the buyer referred us to their friends. I know that Larry and I must have made fifty tips to that little house, but it just goes to show that when you do nice things for people, wonderful things come back to you!

Squirrel

Larry and I have encountered two squirrel attacks to homes. One of the pesky squirrel attacks was in our own home. We went back to the homeland rural Pennsylvania to spend some time with family. At the end of the trip, Larry's sister, Cathy, was asking us to stay one more day, but we could not because we had to get back to work. The trip home was on June 14 which was our son Michael's birthday. The night before we left, Cathy went out and got him a birthday ice cream cake which was so nice of her. Larry's sister, Cathy, is always doing nice things for people, and we love her very much. On the ride home, I was secretly plotting something else special that we could do because it was his actual, I think, fifteenth birthday. When we arrived home around 5:00 p.m. and came through the door, we noticed right away that something was wrong. I first thought that someone broke into the house. The curtains were torn down, the fireplace glass doors were wide open, and then we saw it, *squirrel*. We shrieked. He was hanging on what remained of my family room curtains. I started screaming, "Open the doors. Open the doors," thinking he would run out. It was like something out of *National Lampoon's Christmas Vacation*. He ran back up the chimney, and Larry shut the doors. Now, we had just had the chimney worked on before we left for Pennsylvania, and the guy that did the work left the damper open *and* installed a defective chimney cap. Needless to say, we never used him again. That squirrel chewed every windowsill in nearly the entire house. They were wooden windows, and he tried to chew himself outside. He was a tenacious little creature. What a mess, hunks of wood and squirrel poop was everywhere and, oh, little sooty squirrel footprints on my white dining room chairs and elsewhere.

Michael, Larry, and I spent Michael's birthday cleaning up from the squirrel until midnight. I am ever so grateful to Aunt Cathy getting him that birthday cake!

Larry had to investigate the chimney to see how the squirrel came down, so he had to stick his head into the fireplace. I was terrified because I thought the creature may still be in there and jump on his head. This is when he noticed that the flue was not shut, so he shut it. Every time I walked outside that summer when I would see a squirrel, I would ask it, "Was it you, huh? Did you eat my windowpanes?" I know its teeth were sore because that little squirrel caused twelve thousand dollars' worth of damage, and our homeowners insurance would not pay for it because squirrels are classified as vermin, and our policy did not cover vermin.

That brings me to my next real estate squirrel story. This happened recently on a rental house that we manage for someone living in California. We had the tenant call us, reporting sounds of something in the attic. A lot of scary movies start that way, but instead of calling the ghost hunters, we decided to call a local exterminating company thinking it may be roof rats which are common here in Virginia. The tech got to the house and alerted us to the fact that it was a group of squirrels that chewed a hole into the attic, and they are not allowed to kill squirrels. So we had to call an animal control company to set traps, which they did, and then had a handyman go over to patch the hole. One wily little squirrel did not go into the trap; instead, he chewed his way down the wall and came out behind the tenant's dryer. His friends at the same time rechewed the original hole into the attic. The tenant came home from home and found that the squirrel had eaten all of her bananas and that she was terrified to go to sleep. So the animal control company was called again to set traps in the house. The handyman fixed both holes, and the squirrels were captured. The tenant left a voice mail that she was putting the traps outside. We had to tell the animal guy that he needed to go and pick them up quickly because last summer, a resident of Chesapeake almost went to jail and had to pay a fine because a squirrel caught in a cage expired in his driveway.

Security!

I really hate showing houses with security systems. If it's armed, I am pretty much going to set it off. When Larry and I show property and it has a security system, the first thing that I ask is, "Where is the panel located?"

Agent always says, "It's a piece of cake. It's to the right of the wall when you walk in." And they give you the code.

When preparing to enter one of these houses, Larry and I alert the buyers. We are going into a house with an alarm. If we don't find the control panel, the alarm may sound; if we put the code in wrong, the alarm may sound. OK, pretty much be prepared because the alarm is going to sound. I remember one time in particular, we were showing a house in the Ghent area of Norfolk. Big, fancy house with security system. We went in and heard the beep but no panel to be found. Larry went one way, and I went the other. Still no panel. Let me tell you, those alarms are loud, deafening in fact, not to mention embarrassing. So we looked at the house with the alarm blaring until Larry found the panel down the stairs from the entrance floor in an obscure hallway. We shut it off. Not more than eight minutes total had passed, and I waited on Norfolk's finest to be there in an instant, and they were hands on guns, as I blurted out Realtor and gave them a card. Norfolk policemen do not smile back at you when you set off a security system in Ghent.

Nutria

Those of us living in southeastern Virginia and northeastern North Carolina enjoy a mild climate, beaches, great restaurants, plentiful history, and entertainment. We also share ever-growing numbers of nutria. Nutria are large nasty rodents, and some can weigh as much as twenty pounds. They look like a cross between a beaver and a large rat with big orange teeth. They have little beady red eyes. They look like deranged beavers, and they have been making their way up the coast from Florida. We did not know all of this until several years ago when we went to list a condo that was near a canal in Virginia Beach.

As we were writing up the paperwork, Mr. Seller said, "I guess we should tell you about the nutria that we have here."

We asked what is nutria is, and the seller explained. At the end of the explanation, his wife piped up with, "It's OK, though, because they just lumber on up here and eat the copperheads."

Magic Oil Tank

We once had a very nice tenant with a wife and two small children. When Larry walked them in to the house, he explained all of the functions of the property as we do every single time. This house had an oil heating system. Larry explained that the owner had the oil tank filled for them so that they would have a full tank going into the winter. The owner requested that the tenant leave it full upon moving out. This was in the lease, and the tenant signed it. In the middle of winter, the coldest day of the year, at 11:30 p.m., we got a frantic call from the tenant saying that the hot water heater stopped functioning, and they had no heat. Before I called him back, I thought, *Surely, he had the oil tank filled?* I was almost afraid to ask him the question because I did not want to insult him. So I called him, and he was frantic. So I asked a few questions, and then it got to the point where I had to say, "Sir, when is the last time you had the tank filled?"

He said, "I don't have to fill it until we leave."

I was stunned.

The Haunted Mansion

Let me just say right off that the haunted mansion was really not haunted; it just looked that way. A few years ago, Larry and I received an e-mail from a nice young couple asking about a house in a very exclusive neighborhood in Virginia Beach where some waterfront homes were sold for over a million dollars. The question was, why is this house listed for $499,000? What is wrong with it? So Larry and I decided to preview it for them. This was the largest most horrendously dreadful house we had ever had the displeasure of visiting. It was filthy beyond explanation, and the smell was appalling. Guess what? Someone was actually living there. We never saw them, but we did meet the cat. The poor cat gave out the most distressing m-e-o-w-w-w Larry and I have ever heard. It was like the poor kitty was pleading with us to get it out of there. I could see it in its eyes. *Take me home, please, please, take me home with you, kind Realtor people.* No house from any horror movie I could possibly describe to you could hold a candle to this house. It was truly frightening.

With that being said, it had a great floor plan, great location, an in-ground pool with pool house, and a huge private lot. We had to picture it empty, and then the true beauty of the home came through. We took a million pictures and sent them to the interested buyer with a full explanation of what we found. The entire house needed to be gutted and totally redone. Guess what? They loved it and made an offer, a low one that was accepted. Mr. Buyer made the trip down from New England to be at the home inspection. You can back out on a home inspection for any reason. He loved the house and, more importantly, the neighborhood. I'm sure that the surrounding neighbors turned cartwheels to hear that someone purchased that property and was planning to bring it back to life. They did bring it back to life after many months of hard work. They invited us over to see it, and it is just gorgeous! Larry and I are always delighted to see our buyers so happy!

If I Tell You, You Must Disclose

I was working with a buyer client many years ago while Larry was still on active duty. A house came on the market that I thought he would be interested in. It was a friend of mine that had the listing; we worked in the same office, so naturally I called her to set up an appointment and ask questions about the house.

She said to me, "I know something about that house, but I don't want to tell you because you will have to disclose it to your buyer."

I said, "That is OK, just tell me."

"Well, I really don't want to because if I tell you, you must disclose this information to your buyer."

I said again, "Just tell me." By now, I was really curious. How could I not want to know?

She says, "OK, the owner of the house shot himself and died in the master bedroom."

Yikes. I did not even want to go in that house, but I had to tell my buyer about it. So I told the buyer, and he wants to see it anyway. Oh, boy, so I drove over to show him the house. Everything looked pretty ordinary till we got to the master bedroom. No carpet. It was all taken out, and all around the perimeter of the entire room (and I kid you not), there were hundreds of dead flies. The young man did not buy the house because he didn't like the floor plan.

Pretty Much, if It's Weird,
It Has Happened to Us

In closing the wacky world of real estate, I'd also like to mention that we worked with a young lady that sold her anatomical eggs to science so that she could build a house. While working with buyers, we walked into a house that had a stripper pole right in the middle of the master bedroom. The said young couple bought the house and removed the pole. We sold a house that was condemned by the city of Virginia Beach. I have a picture of the condemned sign on my bulletin board. We met someone that mysteriously kept getting into car accidents to collect money from insurance.

The last conversation I had with this person went like this. "Mrs. Porter, I almost have all the money that I need to pay off my debts so that I can buy a house. I was in another accident, and this one is going to pay big because I broke my ankle *and* I'm pregnant."

She was so excited. Larry and I opted not to work with someone who so enjoyed insurance fraud.

We have never been in a haunted house, but we did show one where its backyard was part of a giant cemetery. Clients have run out of homes screaming though, not because of ghosts but because of flea infestations or roaches. Keep in mind that we live in an area that has thousands of properties for sale at any given time and that Larry and I are usually seeing the house for the first time, right along with the buyer. One time, I showed a vacant townhome (rental) when I was a new agent. I had on white shoes.

After leaving the house and walking to the car, I noticed that my shoes were covered with what looked like pepper. Hmm, pepper doesn't bite. I did what I call the "unhappy dance" batting and swatting at my ankles. You learn a lot of hard lessons real quick in this business.

Oh, and then there is "man's best friend." Larry and I have never been bitten by a dog, yet. Once I threw open a garage door to find a Doberman sitting quietly on the top step waiting to eat someone. I got the door closed in time. One day, as I was about to escort buyers into the backyard of a home, a lovely pit bull greeted us at the door. Agents are supposed to alert their fellow agents about animals. In fact, it is supposed to be stated in the MLS listing; many of them fail to do that. Sometimes, in speaking to an agent, they will say, "Oh just go right in. There is a friendly little dog inside named Sam, and he is very friendly." This is mostly never true.

This is a super nice story. A few years ago, Larry and I had the pleasure of working with Mrs. Smith. She was selling her townhome because her granddaughter was adding an addition onto her home so that both her mother and her grandmother could move in with her. Mrs. Smith told us that she was ninety-five, soon to have a birthday, and that she was on no medications whatsoever. She lived alone and had a little dog to keep her company. She told us that she had a daughter that was in a nursing home, suffering from severe arthritis. Her wonderful granddaughter was now going to care for them both. I loved this lady; she was witty and told amazing stories. When Larry and I would meet with her, I always wanted to stay longer to chat. She is a great inspiration to Larry and me. At the time of this writing, she is still doing well.

One of the strangest things that we have ever seen in a house was a hot tub built into the floor of as master bedroom. It was right beside the bed, *and* there was a shower right next to it. I am not speaking about the master bathroom. These items were actually right in the middle of the actual bedroom.

The hot tub built into the floor reminds me of another house Larry and I showed long ago. This one was a For Sale by Owner. It was as bachelor pad and decorated as such. It was a large house with four bedrooms, 2500 square feet of living space, and it had an in-ground pool. Here in Hampton Roads, we have a room that is referred to as a FROG. It stands for finished room over the garage. The FROG in this house was the owner's man cave. It had a pool table, a huge TV for those all important football games, and a bar (of course) and was decorated with Pittsburgh Steelers memorabilia everywhere. However, this guy's FROG had a really unique element, a urinal, no, not a bathroom with a urinal, as there was no form of a bathroom whatsoever in this space. It was just a urinal, *in a closet.* The closet was carpeted, and the urinal could flush, *but* there was no sink or hand sanitizer to be found. It had a peculiar smell that was kind of like fox pee.

I once opened a door that actually fell off the hinges, making an agonizing thud as it hit the concrete in the garage. Larry and I once showed a home that someone had broken in to. There were pizza boxes in the kitchen, empty and thrown all around. Upstairs, in the master bedroom, we found that this vacant property had an intruder that was camping out in middle of floor making a fire in a bucket. I have no idea how it did not burn down.

We left very quickly since the person/people may have been hiding in a closet and then called the cops and listing agent, in that order.

We have seen items kept in plain sight such as a glass box of diamond rings and necklaces, bottles of pain meds, bongs, handguns, rifles, open safes filled with cash, porn, an entire room full of caged snakes, a cage full of tarantulas, used condoms, a room full of dirty diapers, a pet scorpion, devil worship items and symbols, hoarders (just like the TV show), a guy rebuilding a car engine in the living room, you name it, and we have probably seen it. We once listed a house for some pet lovers. They had four dogs, five cats, four one hundred-gallon fish tanks, two birds, and a four-foot-long monitor lizard and a kennel with five kittens in it that they were taking to the animal shelter. We actually sold that house which was a miracle. Then there was the house that the owner was rebuilding a car engine in the living room. Let's face it; there is never a dull moment in real estate especially when it comes to Larry and I.

We have never had a client die, but we did get a client the house of their dreams because the buyer who submitted a stronger offer than our client died. Our offer was not strong enough, so the seller selected the best offer without asking for a highest and best. Our buyers were heartbroken. The search went on, and one day, we noticed that the home they wanted was back on the market. I called the listing agent, and he informed me that the buyer died in an accident, so the house was back on the market. I called our buyer and relayed the news. His reaction? "Well, I don't rightly know how to feel about that." He and his wife ended up buying that house.

Larry and I have sold homes sight unseen for buyers. I received a call one day from an American service member stationed in Puerto Rico. He said that he found a home on the Internet and asked if I could write up the paperwork for him. At first, I thought it was a prank, but it was actually a serious buyer. It was the last home going up in a new construction site, so I drove out to speak to the site agent. He said, "Let's call him and write it up." So we did. I picked out the carpet color and vinyl selections with his wife on the phone. Larry and I did our due diligence with photos of the house, street, and directed them to neighborhood, school, and police precinct information so that they could make an informed decision. The first time they saw the house was at the final walk through the day before closing. All went well, and the friend that came with the buyer ended up buying and selling two homes with us, and we got to sell the buyer from Puerto Rico's house when they moved five years later. This happens quite a bit now but didn't exist in the late 1990s.

Larry and I were showing houses to a nice young couple that were first-time home buyers. Hampton Roads is such a huge area that there is no way Realtors who work in this area of the country can view every house before they show it. As is protocol, when showing homes, we make an appointment, show up at the appointed time, and then ring the doorbell. Usually, the house is vacant or the sellers leave while the house is being shown. Sometimes, they do not leave. If we do not get a response after the doorbell rings, we use the lockbox that contains a key for entry. So we pulled up to the house, and it looked like a very nice house. Remember the old television series *Tales from The Crypt* from the 1990s? No one answered the door that day, so Larry started to enter the code to open the lock box, just then, and I kid you not, the door opened slowly, and as it did, it mournfully creaked its way open, and it seemed like it took forever. Then we saw the person opening the door, and, honestly, he looked like the host (the scary skeleton guy) from the *Tales from the Crypt* known as the crypt keeper. He was very tall and hunched over and with his daunting voice told us to *please come in*. We just stood there for a moment and then went in, and I remember thinking this guy is going to kill all four of us and bury us in the backyard. We were in and out in an instant.

We once had a home for sale that a talking bird lived in, and his name was Louie. Louie was cool and could mimic the owners' laugh, so, well, you did not know which was which. Louie said a lot of words, and most of the feedback from the house was about how much they like the bird. Turned out that after an exam at the vet, Louie was actually a Louise.

In Closing

There are many people who come and go and make a difference in our lives. A few guide us in ways that will change us forever, making us better for having known them. Larry William Porter and my mother, Rose Clay, are those people for me. As I am writing this, it is just after Easter 2014. Easter Sunday would have been my mother's ninety-sixth birthday. She would marvel at all the technology if she could see it now: cell phones, flat screen smart televisions mounted on the wall, computers in most every home, car navigation systems, and microwave and convection ovens. I'm sad that she did not get to meet her grandson, Michael, and her granddaughter, Terri Lynn (who was born a month after Michael), and not to mention her twelve great-grandchildren, among them my little Beth and Katie-Rose. I know she sees us, but it would have been so great to share all of these loved ones with her. She loved her grandchildren more than anything.

My beauty marks are fading more and more as the years go by. So my mother's prayer really was answered because by the time I'm ready to die, they should be faint, and then when I walk through the gates of heaven, the marks will disappear, and then my mom and I are going to have a big chat, and she will hug me and say, "See, I told you that if you prayed hard enough, the birthmark would go away." And she will be right. I have been asked in the past a question. If you could spend one hour with someone from your past, who would it be? I did not even have to think about it; it would be my mom, Rose Clay.

References

The University of Pittsburgh digital library
The University of Pittsburgh Medical Center
The University of Glasgow
The US Department of the Interior National Park Service of Pennsylvania
Nevus Outreach
CoalCampUSA.com
www.inveraray-argyll.com
Wikipedia.org
About.com
PBS.org
Fayette.pa.us/Historical Perspective
The old miner.rootsweb.com
Ancestry.com
Explorepahistory.com
Secret Scotland.org
The Miami Skin Institute
The Wall Street Journal
Spiritual Mind.com
Virginia.com, Our Great Virginia, John Greenly, retrieved February 17, 2015
azlyrics.com, Blessed, Elton John, retrieved February 16, 20115
metrolyrics.com, This is the Time, Billy Joel, retrieved April 12, 2014
metrolyrics.com, You and Me, Dave Matthews Band, retrieved April 12, 2014
azlyrics.com, Carolina In My Mind, James Taylor, retrieved April 12, 2014

metrolyrics.com, You and Me, Dave Matthews Band, retrieved April 12, 2014

azlyrics.com, I'm Not in Love, 10 CC, retrieved June 12, 2014

azlyrics.com, Sweet Lorraine, Nat King Cole, retrieved, December 21, 2014

azlyrics.com, A Little Help from my Friends, The Beatles, retrieved December 21, 2014

lyricsfreak.com, I Go Swimming, Peter Gabriel, retrieved December 30, 2014

azlyrics.com, This is the Time, Billy Joel, retrieved January 1, 2015

About the Author

L ori Porter is an award-winning Realtor/entrepreneur from
Virginia Beach, Virginia. She is also a devoted mother and
grandmother. She and her husband, Larry Porter, USN
retired, have been in the real estate business for over twenty-two
years. They have helped hundreds of people achieve the American
dream of home ownership.

CPSIA information can be obtained
at www.ICGtesting.com
Printed in the USA
BVHW070833171119
564070BV00001B/143/P

9 781098 009496